Retire Early
Sleep Well

A practical guide to
modern portfolio theory,
asset allocation and
retirement planning
in plain english

SECOND EDITION

Steven R. Davis

Boomer, retired at age 53

Retire Early Sleep Well
A practical guide to modern portfolio theory,
asset allocation and retirement planning in plain english

SECOND EDITION

Steven R. Davis

ISBN: 978-0-9793038-0-7

Published by
Painters Hill Press
P.O. Box 1583
Flagler Beach, FL 32136

Cover design by
Cox & Co.
Black Earth, WI
(608) 767-2181

Printed in the United States of America.

2.0

This publication is designed to provide accurate and authoritative information
in regard to the subject matter covered. It is sold with the understanding
that neither the author nor the publisher is engaged in rendering legal, accounting,
or other professional service. If legal advice or other expert professional assistance
is required, the services of a competent professional person should be sought.

From the Declaration of Principles
jointly adopted by a Committee of the American Bar Association
and a Committee of Publishers

Table of Contents

Part 5 – Retirement

Appendices

Introduction and Preface to the Second Edition

The 1990 Nobel Prize in Economic Sciences was awarded to Harry Markowitz, William Sharpe and Merton Miller for their work in Modern Portfolio Theory. This award was part of a sea change in investing best practices and prudence that has dramatically changed the way big money and smart individuals invest. The retail investment houses have not found a way to profitably share these simple developments with the average investor. So they have obfuscated.

This book brings these developments into the clear light of day, in plain english.

After the recent bear market (2000 to 2002) many investors moved into real estate (which is now clearly not without risk either) or they retreated into very "conservative" asset allocations involving a lot of bonds and money market accounts perceived as less risky. Many have become so "reactionary" in this direction that they will have trouble keeping up with inflation. The simple truth is that it is less risky (and overwhelmingly more profitable) to combine a number of well diversified risky assets together in your portfolio. This is so counterintuitive that most people don't even consider the possibility. The mathematics underneath this principle is so complex (and important) that it won the Nobel Prize. The idea is so simple we can all use it.

This book will show you how. Retire Early Sleep Well is a practical guide to modern portfolio theory, asset allocation and retirement planning. This is a short book, with very short chapters, because the information you need to understand Modern Portfolio Theory and invest for retirement is really fairly simple. If you want to read a lot, check out the references and the suggested reading list (they will allow you to dig into areas of interest as deeply as you wish). You can also find additional materials and resources at *www.retireearlysleepwell.com*.

I've distilled each chapter into an "abstract" at the top of the chapter. I suggest that you start by reading all of the "abstracts" straight through from the beginning. This will provide you with a good introduction to the material as a whole, and provide a helpful context as you read each chapter in detail.

In addition I have provided "navigation tips" at various points to help you navigate to topics of interest (sometimes skipping over sections of the book, sometimes skipping part of a chapter).

A Glossary is included at the end to help you with unfamiliar investment terminology.

Most Americans are living beyond their means and for that reason will not be able to retire in comfort. The average among us are spending every dime they get – and then some. The more affluent are eating out, buying luxury cars and "starter castles." Most seem nearly oblivious of the need to save aggressively to provide the possibility of comfortable or early retirement.

We are faced with a whole generation that has failed to save adequately for retirement, and then in effect "gambling" what nesteggs they have on questionable advice from Wall Street or more personal "crap shoots." We are led to believe that beating the market is a matter of getting the right advice. But research indicates that both professional and individual investors, on average, fail to achieve market returns; and individual investors fail miserably.

Most of the investment advice available from Wall Street and the financial media ignores the developments of modern portfolio theory over the last 50 years. The industry that we turn to for advice about stock picking, market timing and mutual fund picking is very slow to inform us that the overwhelming body of research has discredited these active management strategies.

How can I maximize returns and minimize risk? How can we be assured of reasonable returns and avoid catastrophic losses in the market? How much do I need to retire? How much can I safely withdraw from my nestegg? I wrote this book to save you the trouble of sorting through all the conflicting information out there to develop answers to these simple questions about investing and retirement.

I am not an investment advisor. I am not even an accountant. I'm an architect, but I know the kind of information I needed (and had to work so hard to find and assemble). I have written this book because it just doesn't have to be that hard and because my notes, and outlines of materials were so helpful and useful to friends and associates. They all wanted a **single** book to read, and while many books, particularly the ones on the suggested reading list, are quite good (on some part or even many parts of the subject) not one of them was simple and complete enough for me to recommend alone.

Most of the books about modern portfolio theory are not written in "plain english" and most of the books on retirement planning ignore modern portfolio theory. Retirement planning without modern portfolio theory is dangerous to your wealth.

I eventually satisfied myself that I had answered all my questions and had prepared well for retirement. On August 1, 2001, I retired (at the age of 53), at the beginning of what turned out to be a very difficult period for most individual investors. The elegant power of the simple Nobel Prize winning ideas in this book are fundamentally demonstrated by the fact that my nestegg was not eroded significantly by the three year bear market and then in the recovery proceeded to grow to more than **double** its value since I retired in mid 2001.

This happened in a bear market when many had lost 30%, 50%, 70% or more of their nestegg and were forced to reconsider pending plans for retirement or go back to work if they were already retired. The Modern Portfolio Theory practices recommended by this book protected my nestegg to an utterly inconsequential loss over the three year bear market (-4.8%); and then provided very strong returns of 37%, 17%, 10% and 18% in the four years following.

Too good to be true? No, this experience is common among those who have invested according to these common sense Nobel Prize winning strategies; and the ideas are simple enough that you can implement them yourself or find a reasonably priced financial advisor to help you.

The first edition of Retire Early Sleep Well contained data only through 2001 (two-thirds of the bear market) and none of the subsequent recovery. This new edition reports on the results through the whole three year bear market and four years of recovery. This new data is important because it significantly expands information about the behavior of several only recently tracked asset classes. Many asset classes have been tracked since 1926; some only since 1970 or 1975; and international small cap value and emerging markets only since about 1988. This new data adds significantly to our information.

Before retirement I had been involved in the executive management (and ownership) of large design and construction firms since I was 35 years old. I am a middle-aged boomer who is looking forward to many years of retirement. My wife and I are not among the very wealthy, though we are comfortable. We are not overly worried about the future. Our nestegg is invested well and we sleep well.

What follows is an easy to read, "plain english" guide to investing and retirement based on the Nobel Prize winning strategies of Modern Portfolio Theory and the thrift and sensible savings ethic that made America great.

I hope that you too can   **Retire Early Sleep Well**.

Part One

Retirement Savings
and
Lifestyle Overhead

Chapter 1
Caution - Retirement Ahead

Abstract – The median net worth of households (especially of Boomers approaching retirement) is far too low to provide significant income in retirement.

Retirement is a relatively new concept. Until the last half of the twentieth century retirement was not common. When social security was enacted in 1935, benefits started later than the average life expectancy. Retirement at first was a handful of golden years to be enjoyed in peace, by a small minority of seniors, at the end of a long life of hard work. The idea of 20 or 30 years of retirement is only beginning to be comprehended.

As the baby boomers grow older, the first of them are reaching the age of early retirement. Only those who have built significant nesteggs will be able to retire at around 55 years of age and forgo the last 10 years of the now typical working life. Most of the rest of the boomers will not even be able to retire in comfort at age 65. Many will have to work to age 70 to retire in anything approaching comfort. Real comfort will not be possible for far too many, at any age. Too many are depending too much on Social Security and most have saved far too little, or have no nestegg at all.

> *"There is broad general agreement that America is about to launch an entire generation into retirement without sufficient financial resources to support them. These retirees can expect to live longer, retire earlier, and endure inflation longer than any generation that preceded them. ... There is also broad general agreement that America has one of the lowest savings rates in the world."*
>
> Frank Armstrong, *Investment Strategies for the 21st Century*

The savings rates of most of those approaching retirement are probably inadequate. The total net worth of families in America according to the Federal Reserve Survey of Consumer Finances reveals that net worths are generally far lower than can be expected to support retirement. The net worth of households in America as of 2004 is shown in Table 1.1.

TABLE 1.1   **NET WORTH OF HOUSEHOLDS IN AMERICA IN 2004** (US Dollars)

Age	Median	Top 25%	Top 10%	Top 5%	Top 1%
20 to 29 yrs	$6,000	$30,000	$103,000	$206,000	$607,000
30 to 39	39,000	121,000	272,000	451,000	1,971,000
40 to 49	113,000	353,000	746,000	1,297,000	4,710,000
50 to 59	188,000	570,000	1,180,000	2,223,000	9,554,000
60 to 69	232,000	699,000	1,522,000	3,075,000	10,188,000
70 to 79	183,000	489,000	1,106,000	1,945,000	9,198,000
80 and over	188,000	536,000	1,149,000	1,770,000	3,349,000

The 50 to 59 year olds approaching retirement have a median net worth of only $188,000, and about half of that is tied up in their houses. That means they have only about $95,000 in their retirement nesteggs. In fact, much of the net worth of families with net worths under $500,000 is tied up in their houses. The retirement nesteggs of most families approaching retirement is far too small to allow comfortable retirement.

How is your nestegg doing? How can you accumulate a half million, a million, two million or more? The answer is a little at a time with the power of compounding.

Chapter 2
The Power of Compounding

Abstract - Start early; the power of compounding takes time, but is very powerful. If you wait 10 years to get started, you will have about 1/3 as much at retirement.

Albert Einstein thought that one of his most important contributions was the Rule of 72 (which he is credited with discovering) involving the **power of compounding**. The rule of 72 states that the number of years to double your money at a given return is 72 divided by the rate of return (e.g. 72 divided by 10% = 7.2 years). Compounding is the power at work in the children's object lesson that involves the value of doubling a penny every day for a month. Most are astounded to find that the final value is over $5,000,000 (See Appendix C).

Similarly, the growth of a nestegg's value is deceptively slow in the beginning (but almost spectacular in the out years) underlining the importance of beginning early in investing for retirement. In the table below you can see how the annual investment of $1,000 each year would grow over 40 years (at 10% return).

TABLE 2.1   40 YEAR COMPOUNDED GROWTH OF $1,000

Annual Investment		10 years	20 years	30 years	40 years
$1,000	with no taxes	$17,531	$63,002	$180,943	$486,852

Notice particularly what happens in the out years, between 20 and 40 years, the growth of the investment is quite dramatic; and obviously not mainly from the new money invested each year. Most of the growth is coming from the power of compounding. You can also see how much less you will have if you wait another 10 years to get started with your retirement savings! If you wait 10 years to get started, you will have about 1/3 as much at retirement.

The picture changes dramatically when you introduce the drag of annual taxes on a taxable account. The next table outlines investments of from $1,000 to $10,000 per year in both taxable and tax-deferred accounts.

TABLE 2.2   40 YEAR TAXABLE AND TAX-DEFERRED INVESTMENT PRO-FORMA
Assuming 10% return and 32% total taxes (federal, state and local combined)

Annual Investment		10 years	20 years	30 years	40 years
$1,000	Tax-deferred (IRA)	$17,531	$63,002	$180,943	$486,852
	Taxable	14,617	42,839	97,326	202,523
$3,000	Tax-deferred (IRA)	52,594	189,007	542,830	1,460,555
	Taxable	43,852	128,516	291,977	607,569
$5,000	Tax-deferred (IRA)	87,656	315,012	904,717	2,434,259
	Taxable	73,087	214,194	486,629	1,012,616
$10,000	Tax-deferred (IRA)	175,312	630,025	1,809,434	4,868,518
	Taxable	146,173	428,388	973,257	2,025,231

The lesson: **invest as much as you can in tax-deferred accounts**.

The next chapter outlines your tax-deferred alternatives.

Chapter 3
IRA's, 401(k)'s and 403(b)'s
(The Power of Tax-deferred Compounding)

Abstract – Maximize your contributions to all available tax-deferred accounts.
Always contribute to any level matched by your employer. It's free money!

Everyone should have an IRA, a 401(k), 403(b) or some other of the many forms of tax-deferred savings and retirement plans allowed by the federal government. They provide a **very** significant advantage over taxable investments.

> **Navigation Tip**
> The rest of this chapter contains a lot of details about contribution amounts and rules.
> You can skip over it for now and come back to it when you need particular details later.

Individual Retirement Accounts (IRA's)

IRA investments cannot be withdrawn before age 59½ (withdrawal before then will cost you a 10% Federal penalty). Roth IRA's are taxed differently from traditional IRA's. Traditional IRA's have tax-deductible contributions and taxable withdrawals. Roth IRA's have non-deductible contributions and tax-free withdrawals (the big advantage is that Roth IRA income is entirely tax-free). If you are over 50 you can make additional "catch-up" contributions.

Traditional IRA's. You must start taking Required Minimum Distributions from a traditional IRA by age 70½. Withdrawals are taxed as personal income. If you participate in a 401(k), or other qualified plan, you can still contribute to a traditional IRA. But your contribution will be fully deductible only if your Modified Adjusted Gross Income (MAGI) is less than $52,000 ($83,000 if married); and not deductible at all if your MAGI is over $62,000 ($103,000 if married). If you do not participate in a 401(k), but your spouse does, your traditional IRA contribution is fully deductible only if your MAGI is less than $150,000 (filing jointly); and not deductible at all if your MAGI is $160,000 (filing jointly).

TABLE 3.1	TRADITIONAL and ROTH IRA CONTRIBUTION LIMITS	
	Maximum Contribution	Catch-up Contribution
2006 – 2007	$4,000	$1,000
2008	$5,000	$1,000
2009 on	indexed with inflation in $500 increments	

Roth IRA's. There are no Required Minimum Distributions from a Roth IRA. You can contribute to a Roth IRA if your MAGI is less than $99,000 ($156,000 if married). Above $99,000 AGI ($156,000 if married) your allowable contribution is reduced on a sliding scale reaching zero at $114,000 AGI ($166,000 if married). If you participate in a 401(k), or other qualified plan, you can still contribute to a Roth IRA. A Roth IRA can be passed on to your heirs tax-free (traditional IRA's are taxable to your heirs). The advantages of Roth IRA's are nearly overwhelming – most of you (especially if you are young) will benefit from a Roth IRA.

Educational IRA's. (now called Coverdell Educational Savings Plans) Contributions may be made for children under 18 years of age. Distributions are tax-free if used for qualified educational expenses. The phase out range for individuals is $95,000 to $110,000, and $190,000 to $220,000 for joint filers. The maximum contribution is $2,000 per year.

401(k) and 403(b) Plans

There are many forms of employer-provided plans including 401(k) and 403(b) plans. In 2006, an employee may contribute up to 25% of compensation or $15,000, whichever is less. Many employers match employee contributions (up to some limit), or simply contribute to the plan in the employee's name. Maximum total is $44,000 or 100% of compensation whichever is less.

You should **always** contribute to any level matched by your employer. Where else can you get a 100% (instant) investment return?

Retirement accounts for Small Businesses and Self-employed Individuals

SIMPLE IRA's. Businesses with less than 100 employees (including self-employed individuals) can establish and contribute to SIMPLE IRA's. Both employer and employee can make contributions. The maximum contribution in 2006 was $10,000 plus cost-of-living (COLA) increases, with an additional catch-up contribution of $25,000.

SEP IRA's. Simplified Employees Pension (SEP) plans allow larger contributions, but can only be contributed to by the employer (including self-employed individuals). Catch-up contributions are allowed at the same levels as the 401(k) above. The maximum employer (or self-employed individual) contribution in 2006 is 25% of compensation or $44,000 whichever is less.

SOLO 401(k)'s. For self-employed individuals wanting to shelter more of their income, a Solo 401(k) should be explored. The maximum contribution in 2006 is $15,000 plus 25% of your self-employment income.

Self employed individuals with very high incomes may want to consider a defined benefit Keogh plan to allow very high contributions, especially if you are over 50 and are able to make very large contributions to your retirement program.

KEOGH (HR 10) PLANS. Keogh plans may be either defined contribution plans or defined benefit plans. The contribution limit of defined contribution Keogh plans are the same as the SEP IRA's above.

Keogh defined benefit pension plans are designed to deliver a defined annual retirement benefit, which can be as high as $175,000. The annual contribution depends on your income, the target benefit, years until retirement and anticipated investment returns. Annual actuarial fees and the required IRS report can cost a couple thousand dollars a year; and you are locked into the actuarially determined contribution each year. If your income is high and steady, a defined benefit Keogh plan may be worth all the trouble because it permits far larger contributions than any other plan.

How much will you need to retire? How much will you need to save each year to accumulate that much by the time you want to retire? The next three chapters cover how to budget for retirement, the sources of income in retirement, and provide nestegg rules of thumb (how much you need to be saving for retirement).

Chapter 4
Budgeting for Retirement

Abstract - If you are between 20 and 40 years old, assume your retirement spending will be close to 90% or 100% of what you are making now. If you are between 40 and 50, you can probably use 80% of your current income. If you are over 50, you may be able to use as little as 70% of your current income. Knowing (in detail) how much you are spending now will help. If you plan to travel a lot you may spend as much as you do now - or more!

As you get close to your actual retirement you should budget with some care and accuracy. In order to accurately estimate your post-retirement expenses, you will need to know what you are spending now. There are a lot of good ways to budget and a lot of good software available to help you, like Quicken or Microsoft Money. You will need at least 12 months of expenses, because all months are not created equal. I use the following categories:

Core Budget (Mostly Non-discretionary)
Housing (mortgage, taxes, utilities, repairs and maintenance – or rent)
Food (groceries and dining out)
Automobiles (loans, gas, oil, maintenance and repairs)
Insurance (general liability, life, house, health)
Medical Expenses (not covered by insurance)
Taxes (federal, state and local income & capital gains taxes)
Miscellaneous (the general catch-all; this one gets big)

Discretionary Budget (Possible to decrease in bad times)
Recreation (club dues, green fees, skiing, etc.)
Travel (air fare, lodging, etc.)
Charity (charitable contributions)
Kids (school, general support and bailouts)
Savings and Investment (before retirement)

Think about both a full desired retirement lifestyle budget and a minimum "turtle" (pull back into your shell and ride out a hard time) budget. Both numbers are important to understand.

Some of these budget items will not change much after retirement. Some will change dramatically. Savings and investment will fall to zero. Taxes are likely to be lower. The combination of savings, investments and taxes can add up to as much as a 25% reduction by themselves. Housing, food, automobiles, etc. won't change much. Expenses related to kids will fall, but don't count on anything like zero. Health insurance and medical costs will be very different (often higher, sometimes lower). Travel and recreation can vary a lot, even from year to year (be careful if you hope to travel a lot – it can be very expensive).

Percentage-based rules of thumb are probably a good way to plan retirement spending at a distance of 10 or 20 years from retirement. If you are between 20 and 40 years old, I suggest you use at least 90% of your current income as a place to start. If you are between 40 and 50, you can probably use 80% of your current income. If you are over 50, you may be able to use as little as 70% of your current income. If you plan to be very active and travel a lot more in retirement, you could easily spend as much as you do now – or more! Once you have some idea of your retirement budget, you can begin to explore where the money will come from in retirement.

Chapter 5
Sources of Income in Retirement

Abstract - Sources of income in retirement are limited. If you don't have a pension, you will likely be left with only Social Security and your personal retirement nestegg. Social Security alone will barely get you to the poverty threshold. You need a nestegg! Obviously you can add income from part-time work.

Sources of income in retirement (in addition to part-time work) are limited, in general including only pensions, Social Security and your personal retirement nestegg.

Pensions. Pensions are defined benefit plans, generally provided by your employer (either government or private industry). A defined benefit plan provides a "defined benefit" amount each year, sometimes with an annual cost of living adjustment. Fewer and fewer will have defined benefit plans (pensions) in the future. If you have one, it will still probably not provide all the income you need in retirement, even with Social Security. These plans are relentlessly being replaced by defined contribution plans in private industry.

In a defined contribution plan only the employer's annual "contribution" to your account is defined; whatever it adds up to in the end will become part of your personal retirement savings nestegg. Similarly, you may be able to elect to take your defined benefit as a lump sum, making it part of your nestegg. The alternatives can be very complicated and require careful analysis.

Social Security. Your Social Security benefit will vary dramatically depending on your earnings and when you retire. Social Security benefits are discussed in detail later in chapters 39 and 40. Social Security alone will provide you with the lifestyle of the poor and helpless.

Personal Retirement Nestegg. You need a personal retirement nestegg to provide any income you need in addition to your Social Security benefit. If you don't save for your retirement, you will be left with only Social Security (and any pension). If you don't already have some idea how much you will need in your nestegg, the following chapter will be a big help.

The table below illustrates retirement scenarios for five hypothetical workers with incomes varying from $35,000 to $250,000 per year. For the purpose of the examples, I have assumed that each of the workers needs 90% of that income in retirement and has no pension. The Social Security benefits in this example are from Table 40.3 (for illustration, at age 62).

TABLE 5.1   REQUIRED INCOME FROM NESTEGG (with no pension)

	A	B	C	D	E
Current Earnings	$35,000	$55,000	$90,000	$125,000	$250,000
Retirement Budget %	90%	90%	90%	90%	90%
Retirement Budget	31,500	49,500	81,000	112,500	225,000
Pension	0	0	0	0	0
Social Security (at age 62)	11,560	15,245	17,630	17,630	17,630
Social Security (spouse)	5,780	7,623	8,815	8,815	8,815
Required Income from Nestegg (nestegg withdrawal amount)	14,160	26,633	54,555	86,055	198,555

The next chapter will show you how large a nestegg each of these workers needs.

Chapter 6
Nestegg Rules of Thumb

Abstract - The tables and worksheet in this chapter will allow you to determine how large your nestegg will need to be at retirement and how much you need to be saving each year to meet the goal.

Knowing your required income from your nestegg in today's dollars would be fine if you're going to retire next year. But what about retirement 10, 20 or 30 years into the future? How should you account for expected inflation in your planning?

Let's take the example with the five hypothetical workers a little further and assume that they are each 35 years old, have saved absolutely nothing to date, and want to retire in 27 years when they are 62. We already have their retirement budgets and income from nestegg requirements from Table 5.1 above. To change these withdrawal amounts from current dollars to retirement year dollars we need to multiply by a factor to account for inflation. The inflation factor for 27 years in Table 6.1 below is 2.22 (if we assume 3% inflation).

The inflation factors in Table 6.1 provide the multiplier for $1.00 (in current value) between 1 and 40 years in the future for both 3% and 4% inflation. Most financial planners use between 3% and 4% for planning purposes. In our example I have used 3%.

TABLE 6.1   INFLATION FACTOR

Inflation	3%	4%		3%	4%		3%	4%		3%	4%
Year 1	1.03	1.04	year 11	1.38	1.54	year 21	1.86	2.28	year 31	2.50	3.37
2	1.06	1.08	12	1.43	1.60	22	1.92	2.37	32	2.58	3.51
3	1.09	1.12	13	1.47	1.67	23	1.97	2.46	33	2.65	3.65
4	1.13	1.17	14	1.51	1.73	24	2.03	2.56	34	2.73	3.79
5	1.16	1.22	15	1.56	1.80	25	2.09	2.67	35	2.81	3.95
6	1.19	1.27	16	1.60	1.87	26	2.16	2.77	36	2.90	4.10
7	1.23	1.32	17	1.65	1.95	27	2.22	2.88	37	2.99	4.27
8	1.27	1.37	18	1.70	2.03	28	2.29	3.00	38	3.07	4.44
9	1.30	1.42	19	1.75	2.11	29	2.36	3.12	39	3.17	4.62
10	1.34	1.48	20	1.81	2.19	30	2.43	3.24	40	3.26	4.80

The following summarizes the inflation adjusted income from their nestegg for our five workers.

TABLE 6.2   INFLATION ADJUSTED INCOME FROM NESTEGG

	A	B	C	D	E
Retirement Budget	$31,500	$49,500	$81,000	$112,500	225,000
Required Income from Nestegg	14,160	26,633	54,555	86,055	198,555
Required Income from Nestegg (infl adj)	31,435	59,124	121,112	191,042	440,792

(current dollars times 2.22)

Social Security benefits are adjusted each year to reflect inflation and therefore do not need to be adjusted for this simplified analysis. Your pension, if you have one, may or may not be indexed.

Knowing our hypothetical workers' required withdrawal amounts at retirement will allow us to determine how large each of their nesteggs must be at their retirement. The required future size of nestegg required can be roughly estimated by dividing the required withdrawal amount by a potential withdrawal rate (say 6%). Many would argue that 4% or 5% are safer, but they demand far more aggressive saving. If you can't make a plan that will work at 6% withdrawal, you really don't have a chance; and 6% can work if you are careful (and flexible) in retirement. The analysis in Chapters 37 and 38 indicate that a 6% withdrawal rate is about 95% safe for a retirement period of 20 years; a 5% withdrawal rate is 95% safe for 30 years; a 4% rate is safe for 40 years.

I am inclined to plan on retirement lasting indefinitely (or at least to age 95). You simply cannot afford to outlive your money. Being old and broke is no fun! A 6% withdrawal rate can be sustained if you are flexible in retirement and have a modern portfolio; a 4% withdrawal rate can be sustained under almost any circumstances. I have done my personal planning based on a 5% withdrawal rate; but use 6% in the examples below to illustrate **minimum** savings rates.

You can use this rule of thumb (Nestegg = Annual Withdrawal Amount divided by the Withdrawal Rate) or you can multiply the required withdrawal amount by the factor in Table 6.3 below for each $1.00 of withdrawal (e.g. 16.67 at 6% withdrawal). Or, for a general idea of nestegg size you can interpolate between the amounts in the table.

TABLE 6.3   REQUIRED NESTEGG BASED ON WITHDRAWAL PERCENTAGE

Desired Annual Withdrawal	Required Nestegg at **6%** Withdrawal	Required Nestegg at **5%** Withdrawal	Required Nestegg at **4%** Withdrawal
$1.00	**$16.67**	**$20.00**	**$25.00**
1,000	16,667	20,000	25,000
10,000	166,667	200,000	250,000
25,000	416,667	500,000	625,000
50,000	833,333	1,000,000	1,250,000
75,000	1,250,000	1,500,000	1,875,000
100,000	1,666,666	2,000,000	2,500,000

Continuing with our example we can determine how large a nestegg these five hypothetical workers will need when they retire by multiplying the required withdrawal amount by 16.67 (assuming a 6% withdrawal rate).

TABLE 6.4   REQUIRED NESTEGG AMOUNTS

	A	B	C	D	E
Retirement Budget	$31,500	$49,500	$81,000	$112,500	225,000
Required Income from Nestegg	14,160	26,633	54,555	86,055	198,555
Required Income from Nestegg (infl adj)	31,435	59,124	121,112	191,042	440,792
Required Nestegg	524,025	985,600	2,018,939	3,184,672	7,348,004
(infl adj w/d amount times 16.67)					

Don't confuse your total net worth with your nestegg. If you have a total net worth of $300,000 and $150,000 of it is the equity in your house and cars, you have only a $150,000 retirement nestegg. Your nestegg is your investment portfolio that can be liquidated and spent. You can't spend your house and cars.

How much would each of our five workers need to be saving each year to accumulate the needed nestegg in 27 years? Table 6.5 provides a simple divisor for you to use. The variables in the table are the years to retirement and the investment rate of return. Table 6.5 provides the amount that will accrue in from 1 to 40 years from the investment of $1.00 each year at returns from 8% to 12%.

Historical returns from investment portfolios are discussed in detail later. For now let's just assume they can get 10% per year. For our example, $1.00 invested in each of 27 years will grow to $122.29 at a 10% return on investment. The required nestegg divided by $122.29 yields the amount that must be invested each year to grow a nestegg that size (see Table 6.6).

TABLE 6.5 REQUIRED INVESTMENT AMOUNT DIVISOR
(GROWTH OF $1.00 INVESTED EACH YEAR TAX DEFERRED)

Total Return		8%	9%	10%	11%	12%
Year	1	1.08	1.09	1.10	1.11	1.12
	2	2.17	2.19	2.21	2.23	2.25
	3	3.34	3.39	3.43	3.48	3.52
	4	4.61	4.69	4.77	4.86	4.95
	5	5.98	6.11	6.25	6.39	6.54
	6	7.45	7.66	7.88	8.10	8.33
	7	9.05	9.35	9.66	9.99	10.33
	8	10.77	11.19	11.63	12.09	12.56
	9	12.64	13.20	13.79	14.42	15.07
	10	14.65	15.39	16.17	17.00	17.88
	11	16.82	17.77	18.79	19.87	21.03
	12	19.16	20.37	21.67	23.06	24.55
	13	21.70	23.21	24.84	26.60	28.5
	14	24.43	26.30	28.32	30.52	32.92
	15	27.39	29.66	32.15	34.88	37.87
	16	30.58	33.33	36.37	39.72	43.41
	17	34.02	37.33	41.00	45.09	49.62
	18	37.75	41.69	46.10	51.04	56.57
	19	41.77	46.44	51.72	57.66	64.36
	20	46.11	51.62	57.89	65.00	73.09
	21	50.80	57.27	64.68	73.15	82.86
	22	55.86	63.42	72.14	82.20	93.80
	23	61.33	70.13	80.36	92.24	106.05
	24	67.23	77.44	89.39	103.39	119.78
	25	73.61	85.41	99.33	115.76	135.16
	26	80.50	94.10	110.27	129.49	152.37
	27	87.94	103.57	122.29	144.74	171.66
	28	95.98	113.89	135.52	161.66	193.26
	29	104.66	125.14	150.07	180.44	217.45
	30	114.03	137.40	166.08	201.29	244.54
	31	124.15	150.77	183.69	224.43	274.89
	32	135.08	165.34	203.06	250.12	308.87
	33	146.89	181.22	224.36	278.63	346.94
	34	159.64	198.53	247.80	310.28	389.57
	35	173.41	217.40	273.58	345.41	437.32
	36	188.28	237.96	301.94	384.41	490.80
	37	204.35	260.38	333.13	427.69	550.69
	38	221.70	284.81	367.44	475.74	617.78
	39	240.43	311.45	405.19	529.07	692.91
	40	260.67	340.48	446.71	588.27	777.06

TABLE 6.6 REQUIRED ANNUAL INVESTMENT TO MEET NESTEGG GOAL

	A	B	C	D	E
Retirement Budget	$31,500	$49,500	$81,000	$112,500	225,000
Required Income from Nestegg	14,160	26,633	54,555	86,055	198,555
Required Income from Nestegg (infl adj)	31,435	59,124	121,112	191,042	440,792
Required Nestegg	524,025	985,600	2,018,939	3,184,672	7,348,004
Required Annual Investment (Required Nestegg divided by 122.29)	4,285	8,060	16,509	26,042	60,087
Savings as a % of income	12.24%	14.65%	18.34%	20.83%	24.03%

Very few are saving that much. Those that don't may not reach their goals. They will either have to work longer than they hoped, or spend less in retirement than they hoped – or both! In short, most are living beyond their means. The worksheet on the following page will help you find how much **YOU** need to be saving to meet your goals.

Personal Retirement Planning Worksheet

Years to Retirement

A   **Current Age**   your age today   _____

B   **Retirement Age**   age you want to retire. 55, 62, 65 or 70 (are easiest to use)   _____

C   **Years to retirement**   the only years left to save, invest and grow a nestegg (B minus A)   _____

Current Earnings and Desired Retirement Income

D   **Current Earnings**   total of your earnings and your spouse's earnings today,
in current dollars (not adjusted for inflation)   _____

E   **Desired Retirement Income**   either from a percentage, say 80%, 90% or 100%
of your current earnings or actual budget (in current dollars)   _____

Sources of Retirement Income (other than your nestegg)

F   **Pension** (annual income from pension, part-time work or other source)   _____

G   **Social Security Benefits** from your Social Security Statement
or an estimate/interpolation from Table 40.3   _____

H   **Social Security Benefits** (spouse)
A minimum of 50% of your benefits   _____

I   (non nestegg) **Retirement Income Sub Total** (sum of F+G+H)   _____

Nestegg Income

J   **Income Needed from Nestegg**   the income you need from your nestegg (E minus I)
In current dollars (not adjusted for inflation)   _____

K   **Inflation Factor**   the inflation between now and when you retire (from Table 6.1)
The table has factors for 3% and 4% inflation; use the 3% column as default   _____

L   **Income Needed from Nestegg at Retirement**   (J times K)
In retirement year dollars (adjusted for inflation)   _____

Nestegg

M   **Nestegg Multiplier**   from Table 6.3 for a $1.00 withdrawal at 6%, 5% or 4% w/d rate.
If you're not sure, use 6% for now (16.67).   _____

N   **Nestegg Required at Retirement**   (L times M)
The nestegg you will need when you retire. In retirement age dollars   _____

    O   **Existing Nestegg**
Your total nestegg today, in current dollars.   _____

    P   **Existing Nestegg Growth Multiplier**   from Table 6.7
The multiplier for growth of a $1.00 nestegg with no add'l investments
for the number of years until retirement at a rate of return
from 8% to 12%; if you're not sure use 10% for now.   _____

    Q   **Existing Nestegg at Retirement**   (O times P)
The estimated size of your existing nestegg at retirement
in retirement year dollars, with no additional investments   _____

R   **Nestegg Shortfall**   without additional investment   (N minus Q)
The additional nestegg needed to retire   _____

Investment Required to Eliminate Nestegg Shortfall

S   **Required Investment Divisor**   from Table 6.5
This is the amount that one dollar invested each year would grow to at retirement.
Enter the amount from Table 6.5 that corresponds to the number years to retirement
and the rate of return you expect to achieve in your nestegg portfolio.
If you're not sure, use 10% for now.   _____

T   **Required Annual Investment**   (R divided by S)
This is the amount you need to invest each year until you retire.   _____

U   **Savings and investment as % of earnings**   (T divided by D)   _____
Most people will need to save and invest between 15% and 20%
of their current earnings in order to retire early or well.
If that seems like a lot, read the next chapter on lifestyle overhead!

TABLE 6.7   EXISTING NESTEGG GROWTH MULTIPLIER
(Growth of $1.00 Portfolio with no additional investment)

Total Return		8%	9%	10%	11%	12%
Year	1	1.08	1.09	1.10	1.11	1.12
	2	1.17	1.19	1.21	1.23	1.25
	3	1.26	1.30	1.33	1.37	1.40
	4	1.36	1.41	1.46	1.52	1.57
	5	1.47	1.54	1.61	1.69	1.76
	6	1.59	1.68	1.77	1.87	1.97
	7	1.71	1.83	1.95	2.08	2.21
	8	1.85	1.99	2.14	2.30	2.48
	9	2.00	2.17	2.36	2.56	2.77
	10	2.16	2.37	2.59	2.84	3.11
	11	2.33	2.58	2.85	3.15	3.48
	12	2.52	2.81	3.14	3.50	3.90
	13	2.72	3.07	3.45	3.88	4.36
	14	2.94	3.34	3.80	4.31	4.89
	15	3.17	3.64	4.18	4.78	5.47
	16	3.43	3.97	4.59	5.31	6.13
	17	3.70	4.33	5.05	5.90	6.87
	18	4.00	4.72	5.56	6.54	7.69
	19	4.32	5.14	6.12	7.26	8.61
	20	4.66	5.60	6.73	8.06	9.65
	21	5.03	6.11	7.40	8.95	10.80
	22	5.44	6.66	8.14	9.93	12.10
	23	5.87	7.26	8.95	11.03	13.55
	24	6.34	7.91	9.85	12.24	15.18
	25	6.85	8.62	10.83	13.59	17.00
	26	7.40	9.40	11.92	15.08	19.04
	27	7.99	10.25	13.11	16.74	21.32
	28	8.63	11.17	14.42	18.58	23.88
	29	9.32	12.17	15.86	20.62	26.75
	30	10.06	13.27	17.45	22.89	29.96
	31	10.87	14.46	19.19	25.41	33.56
	32	11.74	15.76	21.11	28.21	37.58
	33	12.68	17.18	23.23	31.31	42.09
	34	13.69	18.73	25.55	34.75	47.14
	35	14.79	20.41	28.10	38.57	52.80
	36	15.97	22.25	30.91	42.82	59.14
	37	17.25	24.25	34.00	47.53	66.23
	38	18.63	26.44	37.40	52.76	74.18
	39	20.12	28.82	41.14	58.56	83.08
	40	21.72	31.41	45.26	65.00	93.05

These calculations assume that all of your investment will be in tax-deferred accounts. This is probably okay because the impact of any taxes will probably be offset by increased earnings (and savings/investment potential) in the out-years.

The worksheet can also be used for any special future needs such as children's education or house downpayment. For many, if not most of us, children's educational needs will preclude full contributions to retirement accounts in at least some years. But if you save less for retirement when you are young, you will need to save more later. This in fact may be a very reasonable choice for many – save a small percentage in your 30's, more in your 40's and more yet in your 50's. A combination of this laddered savings scheme and your naturally higher earnings as you grow older may allow you to reach your goals – gracefully. But don't put off saving!

Table 6.8 below, uses Social Security benefit information from table 40.3 to fill out some of the details of savings and retirement scenarios for our five hypothetical workers at retirement age 55, 62, 65 and 70.

TABLE 6.8   RETIREMENT AGE ANALYSIS FOR FIVE HYPOTHETICAL WORKERS
Current Age 35 (with no nestegg to date)

	A	B	C	D	E
Current Earnings	$35,000	$55,000	$90,000	125,000	250,000
Retirement Budget %	90%	90%	90%	90%	90%
Retirement Budget	$31,500	$49,500	$81,000	$112,500	225,000
Pension	0	0	0	0	0

RETIREMENT AT AGE 55

	A	B	C	D	E
Social Security	11,110	14,690	16,380	16,380	16,380
Social Security (spouse)	5,555	7,345	8,190	8,190	8,190
Total Social Security	16,665	22,035	24,570	24,570	24,570
Required Income from Nestegg	14,835	27,465	56,430	87,930	200,430
Inflation Factor	1.81	1.81	1.81	1.81	1.81
Required Income from Nestegg (infl adj)	26,851	49,712	102,138	159,153	362,778
Nestegg Multiplier (at 6%)	16.67	16.67	16.67	16.67	16.67
Req'd Nestegg at Retirement	447,612	828,693	1,702,645	2,653,086	6,047,514
Req'd Investment Amt. Multiplier	99.33	99.33	99.33	99.33	99.33
Req'd Annual Investment	4,506	8,343	17,141	26,710	60,883
Savings % of Earnings	**12.88%**	**15.17%**	**19.05%**	**21.37%**	**24.35%**

RETIREMENT AT AGE 62

	A	B	C	D	E
Social Security	11,560	15,245	17,630	17,630	17,630
Social Security (spouse)	5,780	7,623	8,815	8,815	8,815
Total Social Security	17,340	22,868	26,445	26,445	26,445
Required Income from Nestegg	14,160	26,633	54,555	86,055	198,555
Inflation Factor	2.22	2.22	2.22	2.22	2.22
Required Income from Nestegg (infl adj)	31,435	59,124	121,112	191,042	440,792
Nestegg Multiplier (at 6%)	16.67	16.67	16.67	16.67	16.67
Req'd Nestegg at Retirement	524,025	985,600	2,018,939	3,184,672	7,348,004
Req'd Investment Amt. Multiplier	122.29	122.29	122.29	122.29	122.29
Req'd Annual Investment	4,285	8,060	16,509	26,042	60,087
Savings % of Earnings	**12.24%**	**14.65%**	**18.34%**	**20.83%**	**24.03%**

RETIREMENT AT AGE 65

	A	B	C	D	E
Social Security	15,945	21,030	24,320	24,320	24,320
Social Security (spouse)	7,973	10,515	12,160	12,160	12,160
Total Social Security	23,918	31,545	36,480	36,480	36,480
Required Income from Nestegg	7,583	17,955	44,520	76,020	188,520
Inflation Factor	2.43	2.43	2.43	2.43	2.43
Required Income from Nestegg (infl adj)	18,425	43,631	108,184	184,729	458,104
Nestegg Multiplier (at 6%)	16.67	16.67	16.67	16.67	16.67
Req'd Nestegg at Retirement	307,153	727,323	1,803,421	3,079,426	7,636,587
Req'd Investment Amt. Multiplier	166.08	166.08	166.08	166.08	166.08
Req'd Annual Investment	1,849	4,379	10,859	18,542	45,981
Savings % of Earnings	**5.28%**	**7.96%**	**12.07%**	**14.83%**	**18.39%**

RETIREMENT AT AGE 70

	A	B	C	D	E
Social Security	20,410	26,915	31,130	31,130	31,130
Social Security (spouse)	10,205	13,458	15,565	15,565	15,565
Total Social Security	30,615	40,373	46,695	46,695	46,695
Required Income from Nestegg	885	9,128	34,305	65,805	178,305
Inflation Factor	2.81	2.81	2.81	2.81	2.81
Required Income from Nestegg (infl adj)	2,487	25,648	96,397	184,912	501,037
Nestegg Multiplier (at 6%)	16.67	16.67	16.67	16.67	16.67
Req'd Nestegg at Retirement	41,456	427,557	1,606,939	3,082,484	8,352,288
Req'd Investment Amt. Multiplier	273.58	273.58	273.58	273.58	273.58
Req'd Annual Investment	152	1,563	5,874	11,267	30,530
Savings % of Earnings	**0.43%**	**2.84%**	**6.53%**	**9.01%**	**12.21%**

Several important observations from the data in Table 6.8:

Reduced savings for later retirement

The later you are willing to retire, the less you appear to need to be saving each year to fund your retirement. But there is a trap. If you decide to save next to nothing and live high on the hog before retirement you are betting on good health and continued good earnings. What would happen if health problems precluded continued work? The answer, you would be forced to depend much more on Social Security and be much poorer in retirement than you were planning for. An aggressive savings program before retirement will **always** give you more freedom and better choices later.

Larger variation in required savings for the average (A) worker

There is a much larger variation in the required savings percentage for the average worker (A) than on the more wealthy (D) & (E). The average worker (A) ranges from 12.88% for age 55 retirement to 0.43% at age 70 (over a thirtyfold difference). The wealthier worker (D) ranges from around 10% to over 20% and (E) ranges from around 12.50% to 25.00% (only about a twofold difference).

The wealthy benefit less from Social Security

On a percentage basis the wealthy benefit far less from Social Security than the average worker. Social Security replaces so much less income for the wealthy workers that their savings must be increased fairly dramatically for any retirement age (vs the average worker). The following table shows the percentage of retirement income each of our hypothetical workers is getting from Social Security at various retirement ages.

TABLE 6.9   **PERCENTAGE OF RETIREMENT BUDGET FROM SOCIAL SECURITY**
(note: the age 55 retirees cannot receive Social Security until age 62)

		A	B	C	D	E
Age	55	48%	40%	27%	20%	10%
	62	50%	42%	31%	21%	11%
	65	68%	57%	41%	29%	15%
	70	87%	73%	52%	37%	19%

If you are not saving 15% you will not be retiring early; and retirement at 55 requires a lot of savings

This table points out that the 15% savings rule works only very generally. It would allow the average worker (A) and worker (B) to retire at 55; worker (C) between 62 and 65; and worker (D) & (E) would have to work past 65 (or retire on less).

To assure early retirement the average worker can save 15%, the more wealthy (C) & (D) workers need around 20% to retire early. The very wealthy (E) requires close to 25% savings.

How much luxury can you afford now and still retire early or well? The next chapter provides some lifestyle overhead analysis.

Chapter 7
Lifestyle Overhead

Abstract -   Lifestyle Overhead (the luxury we consume today) is enjoyed at the cost of reduced nestegg accumulation (meaning later or less comfortable retirement). Live well within your means if you want to retire early.

The luxuries (small and large) that we consume today directly and significantly affect what we will have for retirement.

A $10 pizza each month from age 20 to age 65 will reduce the consumer's nestegg at age 65 by $95,000 (See Appendix C for details).

A $10,000 more expensive car every 5 years from age 30 to age 65 will reduce a consumer's nestegg by $725,000 (See Appendix C for details).

That is **the power of compounding**, and most Americans are not taking advantage of it.

The personal savings rate of Americans has dropped steadily from around 8% in the 70's to near zero (or even marginally negative) today; the results speak for themselves. Only a small fraction of the boomers have any chance for the comfortable retirement that most are hoping for. This is the result of their decision (generally subconscious) to consume now and worry about retirement later. It is a very costly decision! You only have two choices for what to do with every penny of every dollar you earn – **spend it <u>now</u> or spend it (and its compounded earnings) <u>later</u>**.

<u>Navigation Tip</u>
If you are already saving enough, skip the rest of Part 1.

First, stop charging more stuff on your credit cards than you can pay for now. If you are not paying off your credit cards every month, you should cut them up – period! Find a way to live on what you are making and pay off all your credit card debt (work two jobs for a while). Eventually you will have enough to actually start saving.

Second, stop spending every dime you get. If you are not saving, you are living beyond your means – period! The price of a comfortable retirement (or the hope of an early retirement) is simply learning to live well within your means. If you are saving and investing 15% of your gross income you have a reasonable chance to retire comfortably or maybe even retire early if your investments pay off well (or if you turn into a high earner in your out years).

That may sound like a shocking savings goal; to some, it may even sound impossible. It really isn't, but it does require a far lower "lifestyle overhead", than most people realize – not zero, but a lot lower. Think of lifestyle overhead as all the luxuries you consume that are in excess of the minimum required to provide food, shelter and simple clothing. It is a far smaller budget than most people realize. You can revise these numbers for where you live.

TABLE 7.1 THE "BARE MINIMUM" FOR A FAMILY OF FOUR	monthly	yearly
Housing (without any luxury)	$667	$8,000
Food (for simple sustenance)	367	4,400
Transportation (bus or cheap car)	183	2,200
Health Care (health maintenance)	183	2,200
Other Necessities (clothing & misc.)	183	3,200
Total	$1,667	$20,000

The 2006 HHS Poverty Guideline (= basic needs) was $20,000 per year for a family of four. Everything over $20,000 (or a similar level appropriate for where you live) is lifestyle overhead; if the poverty definition is accurate.

So let's adjust that "Bare Minimum" budget up a little to provide some elbow room for comfort – say by 25%

TABLE 7.2 THE ADJUSTED BARE MINIMUM (for 4)	monthly	yearly
"Bare Minimum" Budget	$1,667	$20,000
25% increase	417	5,000
New "Comfortable Bare Minimum" Budget	$2,083	$25,000

Very few of us will choose to live at the poverty level in order to provide for our retirement, but 85% of your gross income is likely to provide for a fair amount of increased lifestyle (luxury). Some lifestyle overhead is reasonable – nobody (well almost nobody anyway) wants to save every penny. But cutting back a little now to allow an early or far more comfortable retirement later is a good trade off.

Looking back at the hypothetical worker examples in the last chapter, remember that the average worker (average according to the Social Security Administration) was earning $35,000 per year and needed to be saving $4,285 per year (12.24% of his earnings) to be able to retire at 62. Lower lifestyle overhead is the only way he can succeed in saving.

TABLE 7.3 ADJUSTED BARE MIN with MAXIMIZED SAVINGS	monthly	yearly
Total Earnings	$2,917	$35,000
"Comfortable Bare Minimum" spending	2,083	25,000
Taxes (assuming 5% state income tax)	400	4,800
Savings and Investments	$433	$5,200
Savings % of Earning		14.85%

I'm not suggesting that it will be easy for the average family to save 15% – it will not. And the peer pressures for all of you will be relentless. Living with less is hard enough for a couple, but kids add a whole new dimension to spending pressure. I can't tell you how many times our kids complained that they "needed" more expensive tennis shoes (or some other of life's necessities). Today, they understand and appreciate what we did together; but at the time, they just thought we were cheap!

If you are borrowing at your maximums (or have unpaid credit card balances), you are living beyond your means – period! Don't let the bank loan officer mislead you! What you can actually afford to borrow is far less than the bank will loan you for your house and car. If you are not saving 15% you are consuming your retirement (or choosing not to retire). You are giving up the freedom to choose retirement, even if you think you will want to continue to work.

Child care costs require a separate analysis. Many two income families would be better off if they forwent the extra income and eliminated all the extra costs (and stress) associated with it. Do the math – **carefully!** It's not just the cost of child care; it's extra transportation, convenience foods, eating out more (because you're tired) – it adds up to a lot more than most two income families realize. If both are high earners, it's another story. But if the second income is a low wage, it may not make much sense.

You will either learn now how to live within your means, with a more moderate lifestyle overhead; or you will be forced to learn in retirement how to live at something far closer to subsistence than you were hoping for.

Chapter 8
Saving

Abstract - If you are not saving enough today, you need to create a savings discipline. Automatic payroll deduction may be just what you need. In addition, you should add part (or all) of your future raises to savings until you reach your saving rate goal.

You already know that you need to be saving for retirement, and once a year you and most other Americans vow to save more next year (and lose weight, eat better and exercise more). On average, very little happens, and the procrastination is very costly (on all counts). We seem to need a missing discipline to trick us into saving.

How come? Well, a new science called behavioral finance tells us that when it comes to savings, investment and retirement planning, we do not behave rationally. We know what we need to do; we just don't do it.

How can we overcome this irrational inertia?

New research by Richard Thaler, of the University of Chicago, points toward a potential solution. **Make the inertia work for you.** His plan involves making enrollment in an employer savings plan automatic (requiring a written request to withdraw from the plan). In addition, employees agree to contribute a portion of all future raises to additional savings (again requiring a written request to reduce additional savings).

Experiments with this plan have produced remarkable results. Enrollment in savings plans increased from around 49% to around 86%; and savings rates increased from 3% of gross salaries to around 11%.

If your employer doesn't offer such a plan, you can still create a similar discipline on your own.

First. If you aren't already contributing to a savings or retirement plan, start contributing at least a little. Whether it's $10 a week, 1% of your gross salary, or the maximum allowed, start savings some amount each week. You can create a significant discipline by establishing an automatic payroll deduction to be deposited to your bank (and transferred to your IRA or other investment account). Check with your employer and bank regarding your options.

Second. Add some of every future raise to this automatic deduction. I suggest you consider adding at least one-third (if not all) of your future raises to savings (until you reach your savings rate goal).

Once you are saving enough, your task then changes to investing it well.

Part Two

Investment Basics

Chapter 9
Capitalism and Free Enterprise
The Engines of Wealth Creation

Abstract -   Capitalism and free markets continue to create new wealth (the world economy is growing); the way to participate is to invest in it (both in the U.S. and in international markets).

Raw entrepreneurship is the real engine of wealth creation.

We all know stories of the spectacular financial success of dynamic entrepreneurs like my last employer, Marshall Erdman. He came to the U.S. from Lithuania in the 30's with $17. He built one of the largest and most innovative design-build companies in the country, amassed a significant personal fortune and provided for the livelihood of about a thousand families.

In every community in the U.S. there are dozens of similar stories of success. "The Millionaire Next Door" documents that there are many, many quiet millionaires in all of our communities both large and small. They are the risk takers in small businesses everywhere.

50% of all the households with a net worth of $1 million to $10 million are business owners; 76% of those with $10 million to $50 million own a business; and 89% of those with more than $50 million own a business. Successful businesses create significant wealth.

These small business opportunities, sometimes started with little more than sweat equity or by risking everything, have the highest rate of return of **all** possible investments; and therefore carry extraordinary risk – the risk of total failure and bankruptcy.

We are lucky to live in America. It truly is the land of opportunity, and the closer we get to its entrepreneurship, the higher our potential returns. I was fortunate to participate in the ownership of several businesses in the last 30 years. Some are no longer in business; some were successful; some were very successful. Those of us lucky enough to have significant ownership in successful small companies have accumulated wealth more rapidly than average.

But all of us can participate in the miracle of capitalism and free enterprise. If you don't have ownership of a small closely held private business, then you should by all means possible (except borrowing) invest in the stock market. Whether we have ownership in a small closely held company, own the publicly traded stocks of corporations in the U.S. and around the world, or simply own mutual funds, we are expressing faith in the growth of the U.S. and world economies.

Over the last 80 years these markets have returned a little more than 7% over inflation. Investments in these markets will form a key part of your investment strategy. But the game has changed in the last 50 years, you can no longer expect to beat the market just because you have the advice of a professional money manager or stock broker.

The academic research of the last 50 years has documented that individuals and professionals alike are failing, on average, to beat the market. The stock picking, market timing and mutual fund chasing strategies of active management no longer work.

Chapter 10
Active Management
The Loser's Game in an Efficient Market

Abstract -   The efficient market theory holds that things have changed in the last 50 years. The market can no longer be beaten by doing research and getting good advice. The market has become well-informed professionals competing with other well-informed professionals and all new information is absorbed immediately. The costs of trying to beat the market cannot be overcome. Trying to beat the market is a loser's game.

Navigation Tip

If you don't want to dig through the research that debunks Wall Street and their stock picking and market timing strategies (active management) you can reread the abstracts in the rest of Part 2 and go on to Part 3, Chapter 18, Modern Portfolio Theory. Come back and read this section later; you need to know this stuff to defend yourself against Wall Street advertising, misinformation and obfuscation.

The conventional wisdom is that the active management strategies of **stock picking, market timing** and **mutual fund picking** are the ways to succeed in investing. They may have worked 30 years ago but they don't work reliably any more. Wall Street claims that this game can be won; but the truth is, it has become a loser's game.

> *"The 'money game' we call investment management has evolved in recent decades from a winner's game to a loser's game. A basic change has occurred in the investment environment; the market came to be dominated in the 1970's by the very institutions that were striving to outperform the market. In just 30 years, the market activities of the investing institutions shifted from only 10 percent of the total public transactions to an overwhelming 90 percent. And that shift made all the difference. No longer was the active manager competing against cautious custodians or amateurs who were out of touch with the market; now he or she was competing with other experts."*

Charles Ellis, The Loser's Game, p 4

In order to compete successfully with these experts, an investor must regularly find mispriced securities to buy or sell at a profit.

> *"The pickers and timers of active management don't believe markets work. They think prices adjust slowly enough that they can systematically uncover incorrectly priced securities and add value beyond added management and trading costs."*

John J. Bowen and Daniel C. Goldie
Prudent Investor's Guide, p 21

Let's look at how quickly markets respond to new information. In **fixed income markets** information is assimilated so quickly that market *"adjustment to announcements regarding interest rates, employment and inflation data begins within ten seconds of the news release and are basically over within 40 seconds of the release."* What kind of chance do you really think you have to get in on that action?

Ederington and Lee,
The Short-run Dynamics of Price Adjustment to New Information
Journal of Financial and Quantitative Anaylsis, March 1995

Research indicates that the **equities markets** are so efficient in incorporating news and announcements into valuations that it is futile to try to beat it. The majority of the price response to overnight news and announcements is realized during the opening trade (for both NYSE and NASDAQ). Valuation adjustments from daytime news and announcements are realized during the first trade following the announcement on the NASDAQ and take only a few trades on the NYSE.

Jason T. Green & Susan G. Watts
Price Discovery on the NYSE and NASDAQ
Financial Management, Spring 1996

Eugene F. Fama coined the phrase "efficient market" in explaining how markets appear to absorb new information so that the current price reflects all known information. Every stock is looked at by at least dozens, if not hundreds, of professionals. Finding one that hasn't already been considered by others is nearly impossible.

> *"In a real way, the very skill, quality and access and number of people doing the research limits the value of the process. ...with so many players, the point of diminishing return may be far behind us."*
>
> Frank Armstrong, *Investment Strategies for the 21st Century*

> *"The securities market is an open, free, and competitive market in which large numbers of well-informed and price-sensitive investors and professional investment managers compete skillfully, vigorously, and continuously as both buyers and sellers. Non-experts can easily retain the services of experts. Prices are quoted widely and promptly. Effective prohibitions against market manipulations are established. And arbitrageurs, traders, market technicians, and longer-term 'fundamental investors' seek to find and profit from any market imperfections. Such a market is considered efficient. ...Not perfect, and not even perfectly efficient, but sufficiently efficient that wise investors will not expect to be able to exploit its inefficiencies regularly."*
>
> Charles Ellis, *The Loser's Game*, p 18

The market is efficient enough that stocks with high expectations have high prices (by any number of measures). The only question is whether the company will do better or worse than expected. In order to make money on the stock, the company must do better than everyone else is expecting (not just do well) in the future. That's often not a good bet. But the market does get exuberant about certain stocks from time to time and a great deal of money can be made (theoretically) by investing in companies for which the news in the future is better than was expected. But that's the rub; the news is by definition random. If you really knew what was going to happen in the future, you wouldn't be reading this book.

> *"In an efficient market, any new information the market receives will be random, not in the sense of being good or bad, but in the sense of whether or not it surpasses or falls short of market expectations. Whether subsequent information will affect the price of a stock in a negative or positive manner is random."*
>
> Larry Swedroe, *The Only Guide to a Winning Investment Strategy You'll Ever Need*, p 65

The fact that stock valuations sometimes move violently does not argue against market efficiency, but rather that new information exceeds or falls short of expectations very significantly. *"The efficient market theory does not claim that the current price is the correct price, only that the market incorporates everything that is known about a stock (including forecasts of future earnings, etc.) into its current valuation or price."*

> Larry Swedroe, *The Only Guide to a Winning Investment Strategy You'll Ever Need*, p 65

Wall Street sometimes admits that most markets are, in fact, fairly efficient, but then claims that small cap stocks, or international stocks, or finally emerging market stocks are traded in relatively inefficient markets. This turns out to be half true, but the cost of trading in these markets is so much higher that the inefficiency doesn't matter. See the discussion of turnover and trading costs that follows in Chapter 13.

The real question is not whether or not the market is efficient or just how efficient it may or may not be. The question is rather, can you overcome all of the costs of trying to beat it. The evidence is overwhelming that neither you, nor most money managers, are able to overcome the costs, and these costs are far larger than most people suspect.

If you listen to Wall Street and the financial media, you get the impression that "beating the market" is simply a matter of getting good advice and applying it. But academic research has shown that most funds and money managers fail to overcome the cost hurdle of transaction costs, fees, and management expenses. In addition, the research has consistently shown that those who do beat the averages do so randomly.

Michael Jensen was among the first to look carefully at the performance of mutual funds. He studied the performance of 115 mutual funds from 1945 to 1964. He published studies in 1968 and 1969 documenting the risk adjusted performance of these funds (56 funds had data back to 1945; all 115 had data from 1955 on). Jensen utilized the concept of "alpha" to measure risk-adjusted performance. Alpha is a measure of the return of a fund in excess of a benchmark. A negative alpha is underperformance.

> *"It appears from the preponderance of negative alphas that the funds were not able to forecast security prices well enough to recover their research expenses, management fees and commissions."*
>
> Michael Jensen, *The Performance of Mutual Funds from 1945-1964*, Journal of Finance, May 1968 p 406

> *"One must realize that these analysts are extremely well endowed. Moreover, they operate in the securities market every day and have wide ranging contacts in both the business and financial communities. Thus, the fact that they are apparently not able to forecast returns accurately enough to recover their research and transaction costs is a striking piece of evidence in favor of the strong [efficient market] hypothesis."*
>
> Michael Jensen
> *Risk, the Pricing of Capital Assets, and the Evaluation of Investment Portfolios*
> Journal of Business, April 1969, p 170

Far fewer mutual funds beat their benchmarks each year than we are led to believe, and to make matters worse their past performance doesn't seem to matter. The next chapter looks at the actual performance of mutual funds.

Chapter 11

Actual Mutual Fund Performance and Persistence of Performance
(good past performance does not persist into the future)

Abstract -   Research indicates that very few mutual funds beat their benchmarks each year, that those doing so appear to be random, and that good past performance does not persist into the future. Nobody can guess which mutual funds will do well in the future. On average, mutual funds trail their benchmarks by the total of all their costs and expenses.

Each year there is new list of the best mutual funds (from last year). If there was strong persistence of past performance into the future, these lists would look a lot more alike year after year. The painful truth is that these lists are almost useless, because next year it's going to be a whole new bunch.

The fact that nearly **one-third** of the mutual funds existing since 1961 have disappeared is not mentioned in the ads. The fact that "average" surviving mutual fund performance is increased due to the exclusion of these "dead" funds from the data is not mentioned in any ads. When a mutual fund is doing so badly that it cannot recover, it ceases business either by dissolving or being absorbed into other funds in a group. Survivorship bias (the upward bias of returns data because of the exclusion of failed funds) is a term of the scholarship of finance. It is one of Wall Street's secrets.

A landmark study by Mark Carhart reviewed the performance of all known equity funds (adjusted for survivorship bias) from 1962-1993. His data set included 1,892 funds. From 1962 to 1993, 582 of the funds had disappeared. Carhart concluded:

> "... that persistence in mutual fund performance is almost totally explained by differences in fund expenses and transaction costs, rather than the superior stock picking or market timing skills of the managers."

> "Winners are somewhat more likely to remain winners, and losers are more likely to remain losers or perish. However, the top decile [the best performing 10% of the funds] differ substantially each year, with **more than 80% turnover** in their composition. In addition, **last years winners frequently become next years losers and vice versa**, which is consistent with **gambling behavior** by mutual funds."

> "... the year to year rankings of most funds appear to be random."

> "Funds in decile 1 [the best 10% of funds] have a 17% probability of remaining in that decile, and the funds in decile 10 [the worst 10% of funds] have a 46% chance of remaining in decile 10 or disappearing from the sample altogether."

Mark M. Carhart
On Persistence in Mutual Fund Performance
Journal of Finance, Mar 97

Mutual Fund ratings such as Morningstar's Star System don't predict future performance. A Lipper Analytical Services study of only Morningstar 5 star funds found that 90 of 94 would have failed to beat the portfolio asset classes.

> Larry Swedroe, *The Only Guide to a Winning Investment Strategy You'll Ever Need*, p 29

"The connection between past and future performance has not been firmly established by stars, historical star ratings, or any raw data"

> John Rekenthaler,
> editor of Morningstar Mutual Funds
> quoted by Swedroe, *The Only Guide to a Winning Investment Strategy You'll Ever Need*, p 29

"We never intended to suggest that the stars could be used to predict short term returns or to time fund purchases. They were just a way to sort funds according to past success"

> Morningstar Mutual Funds, 12/8/95
> quoted by Swedroe, *The Only Guide to a Winning Investment Strategy You'll Ever Need*, p 29, 30

"It is estimated that 80% of new fund purchases are four and five star ranked funds. Apparently, not many investors know that Morningstar ratings have no predictive value"

> Kipplinger Personal Finance, Feb 97
> quoted by Swedroe, *The Only Guide to a Winning Investment Strategy You'll Ever Need*, p 30

Michael Jensen, in his 1969 study, found **no** significant evidence that *"a fund manager who experienced superior performance in the earlier period was far more likely to experience superior results in the later period."* On the other hand, he did find that *"a fund which was inferior in the earlier period was very likely to be inferior in the later period."* He then continues with an observation that caused me to laugh out loud (very rare in the stacks of the UW Business School):

> *"This result is not too surprising, since it is very simple to consistently hold an inferior portfolio. In the absence of forecasting ability all one need do is generate substantial expenses through time to insure inferior performance"*

> Michael Jensen
> *Risk, the Pricing of Capital Assets, and the Evaluation of Investment Portfolios*
> Journal of Business, April 1969, p 236

The negative contribution of expenses can hardly be overemphasized. Carhart observes that *"mutual fund managers claim that expenses and turnover do not reduce performance, since investors are paying for the quality of the manager's information, and because managers trade only to increase expected returns net of transaction costs."* That's their claim anyway; their results appear to indicate that they are overconfident. He found that their *"expense ratios, portfolio turnover and load fees are significantly and negatively related to performance."*

> Mark M. Carhart
> *On Persistence in Mutual Fund Performance*
> Journal of Finance, Mar 97, p 80

The next chapters look by turn at the costs associated with operating expenses, turnover and trading costs, the index fund advantage and distributions and taxes.

Chapter 12
Mutual Fund Operating Expenses

Abstract - Mutual fund operating expenses are a serious drag on their performance. The higher the expenses the poorer the performance. Index funds have the lowest expenses possible and therefore come closest to their benchmarks.

Proponents of active management claim that informed investors (mutual fund managers in particular) earn enough to compensate for the cost of gathering and analyzing information. These expenses are reflected in their published expense ratios. But Mark Carhart found that:

"Most funds underperform by about the magnitude of their investment expenses. The bottom decile funds [the worst 10% of funds], however, underperform by about twice their reported investment costs.

> Mark M. Carhart
> *On Persistence in Mutual Fund Performance*
> Journal of Finance, Mar 97, p 80

The Elton and Gruber study of 143 mutual funds from 1965 to 1984 showed a strong inverse relationship between cost and performance. The benchmark for each fund was a portfolio of indexes reflecting each fund's individual exposure to S&P 500, small cap and bonds. The resulting "alpha" for each fund reflects their risk adjusted performance compared to the fund benchmark. Not only did the funds as a whole underperform the indexes, the more expensive the fund is, the worse it performs.

TABLE 12.1   ELTON & GRUBER   EXPENSE vs. PERFORMANCE

Quintile	Expenses	Alpha
5 (high)	0.912 to 2.020	-3.87%
4	0.753 to 0.912	-1.68%
3	0.680 to 0.753	-0.69%
2	0.590 to 0.680	-1.19%
1 (low)	0.000 to 0.590	-0.59%

> Edwin J. Elton, Martin J. Gruber, et al
> *Efficiency with Costly Information*
> Society for Financial Studies, 1993

The facts are simple, fund expenses have a negative impact on fund performance, the higher the expenses, the worse the performance. Index funds have lower expenses because they are not trying to beat the market; they simply buy and hold the market (or market segment) and therefore perform closer to their benchmarks.

Solution – find the index fund (for the asset class you want to hold) with the lowest expenses.

In addition to operating expenses, some funds charge 12b-1 fees, front-end loads or deferred sales charges. Be careful to understand all of these fees and loads – they cost you real money. Since load funds have not out-performed no-load funds, there is no good reason to pay these fees and loads. There are plenty of good no-load funds available to choose from.

The only exception is the fee for redemption in less than three to five years that some funds use to limit trading and attract buy-and-hold investors.

Chapter 13
Turnover and Trading Costs

Abstract - The trading costs associated with the turnover of mutual funds is an important (unreported) overhead for the funds. In addition, higher turnover is directly related to poorer performance. The trading costs in small cap funds are particularly high. Active management only makes things worse. The average turnover of actively managed mutual funds is 85%; the turnover of passively managed index funds is typically less than 10%.

Active fund managers (the stock pickers and market timers) do a lot of trading. The average retail mutual fund has a turnover rate of 85%; which means that they replace 85% of their holdings each year with new holdings.

High turnover is costly to fund shareholders because of the trading costs associated with commissions, bid-ask spreads and market impact costs. These costs are a hidden drag on the performance of a mutual fund – in addition to its published expenses. Trading costs for small cap stock funds can exceed management fees. While less for large cap stock funds, they are always significant.

Trading costs are closely related to the bid-ask spread, the difference between the asking price (the price at which a stock is bought by a broker for an investor) and the bid price (at which it is sold by a broker to an investor). This "spread" is the fee charged by the market makers; it is their overhead and profit – the cost of liquidity in our markets.

The trading volume for large cap stocks like IBM, GE and Walmart is very high (very many trades each day), so the profit and overhead for each trade remains very small (they make it up in volume). But the volume of trading for relatively unknown and unfollowed small and micro cap stocks is very low (sometimes no trades at all in a given day), so the profit and overhead for each trade is far higher (there is no volume to make it up on).

The bid-ask spread is nearly 12 times greater for stocks in the smallest CRSP (Center for Research on Securities Pricing) decile than for the largest decile. CRSP deciles represent the whole market divided by size according to market capitalization. See Chapter 23 for additional details regarding CRSP deciles.

TABLE 13.1	U.S. MARKET BID-ASK-SPREAD
Decile	Bid-ask-spread
1 (large cap)	0.53%
2	0.60%
3 (mid cap)	0.71%
4	0.98%
5	1.25%
6 (small cap)	1.26%
7	1.61%
8	2.21%
9 (micro cap)	2.99%
10	6.19%

The bid-ask spreads in international markets are even higher.

As a rule-of-thumb you can estimate the trading cost of a fund by multiplying its turnover rate by its average bid-ask spread (the percentage spread for its average size holding). For the average mid-cap fund this amounts to

> 85% turnover x 1.25% bid-ask spread, or a **1.08%** drag on performance **in addition to its published expenses!**

The turnover in index funds is far smaller, ranging from 1% to no more than 25%, depending on the asset class – say 10%.

> 10% turnover for passive funds x 1.25% bid-ask-spread would be only **0.125%** (1/8 of one percent instead of over one percent)

The average trading costs for active, passive, large, mid and small cap funds may be summarized as follows. The following estimates of trading costs are based on an average active turnover of 85% for active funds and 10% for passive index funds, and the bid-ask spreads from the table above.

TABLE 13.2   ESTIMATES OF TRADING COSTS FOR FUNDS

	Bid-Ask Spread	ACTIVE 85% turnover	PASSIVE INDEX 10% turnover
Deciles 1&2 (large cap)	0.57%	85%x0.57%= **0.48%**	10%x0.57%= **0.06%**
Deciles 3-5 (mid cap)	0.98%	85%x0.98%= **0.83%**	10%x0.98%= **0.10%**
Deciles 6-8 (small cap)	1.61%	85%x1.61%= **1.37%**	10%x1.61%= **0.16%**
Deciles 9-10 (micro cap)	4.59%	85%x4.59%= **3.90%**	10%x4.59%= **0.46%**

These differences form a significant hurdle for active managers. Most fail to clear it.

In addition to paying the bid-ask spread, a large trade (one that is a significant percentage of the daily trading volume of a stock) is likely to influence the price. This market impact cost adds additional cost to the transaction (making winners more expensive to buy and losers into bigger losers).

The Elton and Gruber study of mutual funds also showed an inverse relationship between turnover and performance – the higher the turnover, the worse the performance.

TABLE 13.3   ELTON & GRUBER   TURNOVER vs. PERFORMANCE

Quintile	Turnover	Alpha
5 (high)	72% to 162%	-2.21%
4	51% to 72%	-1.87%
3	34% to 51%	-2.17%
2	22% to 34%	-1.11%
1 (low)	0% to 22%	-0.58%

Edwin J. Elton, Martin J. Gruber, et al
Efficiency with Costly Information
Society for Financial Studies, 1993

In addition, heavily advertised high turnover funds penalize buy-and-hold investors. The "hot money" that chases last year's returns and then sells on any "alarming" drop in value, can sell at net asset value – effectively free from the long term costs of high turnover. Long term buy-and-hold investors are left holding the bag.

The facts again are simple. High turnover has a negative impact on fund performance. The solution – find the index funds with the lowest possible turnover and fees.

Chapter 14
The Index Fund Advantage

Abstract - The low expenses, trading costs and impact costs of index funds provide a huge advantage.

There's a lot more to index funds today than the S&P 500 funds that dominate attention. The Vanguard 500 Index Fund is today the largest mutual fund in the world, and there are numerous other S&P 500 index funds available. The S&P 500 is by far the most popular index around which index funds are constructed, and it remains an important proxy for the market as a whole.

But there are many other kinds of index funds, and numerous other indexes around which new funds are being built each year. Individuals now have available to them numerous index funds that track all manner of important segments such as small cap, value, international and emerging markets.

The first index fund (started in 1971) was available only to institutional investors. Other institutional funds followed in 1973, and then in 1975 John Bogle and the Vanguard Group offered the first retail index fund to individuals.

The growth of indexing since then has been in response to strong and growing demand for alternatives to the failed active management strategies of most mutual funds. The index fund advantage is that, in addition to broad market diversification, it assures at least very close to market returns by minimizing the expenses involved in mutual fund investing.

The following table compares the expenses of both actively managed mutual funds and index funds in three important general asset classes.

TABLE 14.1   ACTIVE FUND VS INDEX FUND EXPENSES

	Large Cap	Small Cap & Int'l	Emerging Markets
Active Fund Expenses			
Expenses Ratio	1.30%	1.60%	2.00%
Trading Costs	0.48%	1.37%	3.00%
Impact Costs	0.30%	1.00%	3.00%
Total Active Fund Expenses	2.08%	3.97%	8.00%
Index Fund Expenses			
Expenses Ratio	0.17%	0.27%	0.57%
Trading Costs	0.06%	0.16%	0.40%
Impact Costs	0.02%	0.15%	0.40%
Total Index Fund Expenses	0.25%	0.58%	1.37%
The Index Fund Advantage	1.83%	3.39%	6.63%

The total expenses of actively managed funds are a significant headwind against which active managers constantly strain. Their failure to demonstrate stock picking or market timing skills adequate to recover these costs is now well documented.

The solution – index funds.

Chapter 15
Distributions and Taxes

Abstract - Individual taxes (income and capital gains taxes) on mutual fund distributions can cause your personal return from a fund to be far lower than its published return (sometimes by a lot). Taxable investment performance must be evaluated on an after-tax basis. Taxes are not an issue in an IRA, 401K or other tax-deferred account.

Mutual funds must distribute 98% of their taxable income each year (or pay huge additional taxes). The resulting distributions create taxable income for fund shareholders in the form of dividends, interest and capital gains. This is very important for your taxable investment accounts. But funds do not tend to publish much after-tax data, because it is such bad news!

Studies indicate that the average taxable investor in actively managed funds (who reinvests all distributions) ends up with only 45% to 55% of a fund's published performance after taxes.

> John B. Shoven and Joel M. Dickson
> *Ranking Mutual Funds on an After Tax Basis*
> Stanford University Center for Economic Policy
> Research, Discussion Paper #344

Robert Jeffrey and Robert Arnott's study compared the after-tax performance of actively managed mutual funds with a passively managed index fund. They found that 21% of the funds, 15 out of 72, outperformed the index fund on a pre-tax basis; but only 7%, 5 out of 72, outperformed the index fund after taxes were accounted for.

> Robert H. Jeffrey & Robert D. Arnott
> *Is Your Alpha Big Enough to Cover Your Taxes*
> Journal of Portfolio Management, Spring 93

Subsequent reductions in capital gains tax rates have improved the situation marginally, but taxes remain an important problem for mutual fund investors.

There are horror stories involving distribution and taxes from actively managed mutual funds. Often they involve paying taxes on large distributions while the fund's value has declined. This problem could be exacerbated in a major market crash when a fund must liquidate highly appreciated assets to cover withdrawals. In addition, to assure adequate liquidity for the fund during panic selling, the funds tend to keep cash on hand that dilutes their returns.

You should stay away from heavily advertised funds that attract the "hot money" that is likely to panic in the next downturn and cause you to "receive" large unexpected distributions.

Passively managed funds will generally have far lower distributions. Passively managed funds will always have lower turnover, and that will make their distributions much more stable and predictable. With active managers, you never know when unrealized gains will be realized.

Taxes are not an issue inside an IRA or other tax-deferred account. In these accounts, you can use tax-inefficient funds without penalty.

Chapter 16

Actual Results of Individuals
(much poorer than you think)

Abstract - Over the last 20 years, individuals, on average, have earned only about 4% per year while the funds they invested in were earning about 12% per year. This poor performance is directly related to bad market timing – chasing the hot funds and panic selling in market declines. Individuals also do poorly as traders of common stocks. On average, the stocks they sell do better than the new stocks they buy after the trade. They would do far better with a simple buy-and-hold strategy, instead of their buy high sell low behavior.

The average individual investor is overconfident – period!

Investors don't want to admit it, but they are not doing well in the market. Studies indicate that individuals owning shares in mutual funds are earning only a very small fraction (20% to 35%) of the published returns of the funds themselves. What in the world are they doing? How can anyone do THAT bad?

In 1994 Dalbar Financial Services conducted an analysis of results of individual investors in mutual funds as opposed to the published results of the funds themselves. The original *Quantitative Analysis of Investor Behavior* (The QAIB) covered the period from 1984-1993. The QAIB study has been regularly updated since then and continues to document the awful performance of individuals in mutual funds. Dalbar's summary of the 2006 update states that in the period from January 1986 to December 2005 the average equity fund investor realized an annualized return of 3.9%, compared to 11.9% for the S&P 500 index fund. **The average individual trailed the index by 8%.**

> *$1,148 total return on $1,000 for individuals (over 20 years), when there was $7,475total return on $1,000 of S&P 500 over the same period (7.37 times more!)*

But that is only part of the bad news. The real situation is far worse. Inflation across this period was 3.0% leaving only a 0.9% real return for the average individual against an 8.9% real return for the S&P 500; that is:

> *$196.25 real growth on $1,000 for individuals (over 20 years), when there was $4,502.47 growth on $1,000 of S&P 500 over the same period (22.94 times more!)*

This extremely poor performance is directly related to bad market timing and short holding periods. Individuals overreact to changing market conditions. And the more an investor buys and sells, the lower the returns.

The QAIB also tracked money flowing into and out of mutual funds and measured the length of time investors remained invested in them. Individuals average fund retention was 4.3 years in 2005 (the highest level in 20 years, up significantly from 1.7 years after the stock market crash in 1987). Returns for investors clearly illustrate that they would have benefited from a buy-and-hold strategy. The data indicates that investors invariably buy high and sell low. AFTER the market goes up, cash flows in. AFTER the market goes down, cash flows out.

Stephen Nesbitt looked at individual investments in mutual funds over a 10 year period. He found that despite good performance records for the mutual funds over the period, poor timing of cash flows reduced returns to investors.

"Mutual fund cash flows repeatedly go to asset classes near their performance peaks, and leave quickly after returns level off or fall. Unfortunately, the investment industry contributes to this result by heavily advertising products with favorable short term performance."

Stephen Nesbitt,
Buy High, Sell Low: Timing Errors in Mutual Fund Allocation
Journal of Portfolio Management, Fall 1995, pp 57-60

Investors tend to form a humongous herd that drives the prices of high performing stocks to unrealistic highs and poor performing stocks to unrealistic lows. Investors seem to have an uncanny ability to buy high and sell low.

Terrance Odean analyzed the detailed trading records for a large sample of investors (66,000 households) from a discount brokerage house. **The stocks that individuals sell subsequently outperform the stocks that they buy**.

Terrance Odean, *Why Do Investors Trade So Much?*
Working Paper, 1977

In a study published later regarding the same data, he looked at the trading behavior and success of these individuals from 1987 to 1993. He found that trading by individual investors was excessive and dysfunctional. He divided the group into quintiles by trading volume. The average household had an annual turnover of 75%. The highest trading quintile had a turnover of over 250%!

"Those that trade most earn an annual return of 11.4%, while the market returns 17.9%. ...Overconfidence can explain high trading levels and the resulting poor performance of individual investors."

Terrance Odean and Brad Barber
Trading is Hazardous to Your Wealth
Journal of Finance, April 2000

In 1995 Morningstar was commissioned by Fundminder, Inc. to evaluate investor returns from mutual fund investments. *"The study evaluated 199 growth mutual funds for which they had performance data for 1989-1994. The average return for the 199 funds over the six year period was 12.01 %. So, how did the individual owners of those same 199 funds do for their various periods of ownership? Not good. The average annualized return was just 2.02%! They turned 12% returns into 2% returns!"*

John Merrill, *Beyond Stocks*

Either market timing or chasing the hot manager turned their 12 percent return into 2 percent. Buy high, sell low!

"Further proof of this finding was provided by Peter Lynch, the highly regarded manager of the Fidelity Magellan Fund during its glory years, who told an audience of investment advisors in 1992: 'Over half of my investors in Fidelity Magellan during my tenure at the helm lost money due to poorly timed buy and sell decisions.' This despite Magellan being the number one performing mutual fund over those 10 years!"

John Merrill, *Beyond Stocks*

If buying low is such a good idea, how come so few people do it?

The stock market may well be the only "store" where we refuse to buy good stuff when it's on sale and then greedily buy it up when the price goes back up. If you can buy $1.00 bills for 75 cents, who in his right mind would wait until they cost $1.25. A down markets means long-term bargains! You need to get used to the idea that there are going to be down markets, sometimes for extended periods. The overreaction of individuals to market conditions has been (and for most will continue to be) very costly. If you are adequately diversified into a number of good low cost index funds, you can rebalance your investments at the end of each year and in effect buy low and sell high (Chapter 37 contains a discussion of rebalancing).

Chapter 17
Wall Street Misinformation
Technical and Fundamental Analysis

Abstract - Wall Street and the financial media are still selling active management – stock picking, market timing and mutual fund picking. Their obfuscation of their failure is relentless. Neither fundamental security analysis nor technical analysis works. These guys are guessing, and on average they seem to be right less than half the time, but you will still pay dearly for their advice. Warren Buffet and Peter Lynch both recommend index funds.

Wall Street and the media continue to sell advice about stock picking, market timing and mutual fund picking even though the overwhelming body of research has discredited these strategies. They continue to pander to investors who hope to beat the market by finding the next Microsoft (or the next Warren Buffet or Peter Lynch), or timing the next market moves, up or down. The investment pandering that encourages this hope is shameless and self-serving.

The stock broker calling you with his latest "tip" is not your friend.

> *"Don't be confused about stockbrokers. They are usually very nice people, but their job is not to make money for you. Their job is to make money from you."*

> *"The typical stockbroker 'talks to' 200 customers with invested assets of $5 million. To earn $100,000 a year, he needs to generate $300,000 in gross commissions, or 6% of the money he talks to."*

> Charles Ellis, *The Loser's Game*, p 105

Wall Street maximizes its profits in a number of ways; many do not benefit investors. Buy recommendations far exceed sell recommendations on Wall Street. Why?

> *"There is a darker side to the research problem that investors must also consider. Conflicts of interest can easily creep into analysis. It shouldn't surprise us that buy to sell recommendations is skewed, and that sell recommendations come far too late to be of any use."*

> Frank Armstrong, *Investment Strategies for the 21st Century*, ch 7

The main reason that the majority of individual investors don't know about the last 50 years of research and modern portfolio theory is that the primary business of the financial media is not educating the public; but rather, maximizing their profits. Their advertising revenue comes mainly from financial advisors and mutual funds hawking their stock picking and market timing skills.

Numerous studies of the lists of "the best mutual funds" confirm that they are useless – or worse. The obvious question – why is it a new list every year – remains unanswered. Studies indicate that following this kind of advice is hazardous to your financial wealth.

> *"I believe the search for the top performing stock funds is an intellectually discredited exercise that will come to be viewed as one of the great financial follies of the late 20th century"*

> Jonathon Clements,
> Wall Street Journal, Apr 29, 1997
> quoted by Swedroe, *The Only Guide to a Winning Investment Strategy You'll Ever Need*, p 38

Stories of wildly profitable stock picks, market timing calls and mutual funds amount to investment pandering. But that is all you can find in the financial media.

> *"Americans are indulging themselves in investment porn. Shameless stories about performance tickle our prurient financial interest."*
>
> Jane Bryant Quinn, Newsweek, 8/7/95

Wall Street research comes in two basic flavors: technical analysis and fundamental analysis. Neither of these reliably works.

Technical Analysis

Technical analysts used to be called "chartists," but that title has been abandoned. Wall Street uses them to generate trading volume even though most of their "science" has been thoroughly discredited. Some technical analysts, especially those associated with hedge fund strategies, have demonstrated important success; but almost no individuals have the mathematical or statistical skills or computer systems and data bases to compete with these professionals. Importantly, the anomalies they take advantage of disappear quickly (sometimes in minutes or hours). This stuff is of no use to most of us.

Fundamental Analysis

Fundamental analysis is more scientific, but it is still useless for forecasting. Benjamin Graham, the father of fundamental analysis, was interviewed shortly before his death in 1976. Benjamin Graham and David Dodd authored Security Analysis, the bible of fundamental analysts to this day. In the interview he said the following:

> *"I am no longer an advocate of elaborate techniques of security analysis in order to find superior value opportunities. This was a rewarding activity, say forty years ago when our textbook 'Graham and Dodd' [Security Analysis] was first published; but the situation has changed a great deal since then. In the old days any well-trained security analyst could do a professional job of selecting undervalued issues through detailed studies; but in the light of the enormous amount of research now being carried on, I doubt whether such extensive efforts will generate sufficiently superior selection to justify their cost."*
>
> Benjamin Graham Interview
> Financial Analysts Journal
> September/October 1976

A study by two academic researchers found that only 13 of 237 market timing newsletters survived the 12.5 year period of their study.

> W. Scott Simon, Index Mutual Funds

The Wall Street Journal conducts a biennial survey of the nation's top Wall Street and professional economists. For the 18 years from 1969 to 1997: 3-mo. T-Bills moved in the opposite direction of the consensus forecast 53% of the time; 30-year Bond consensus was wrong 67% of the time. The more rates moved, the worse the forecasts got (essentially, economists missed 9 of the 10 largest moves in the last 18 years). Only 14 of the 44 (who participated in at least 10 surveys) guessed the right direction 50% of the time; none were accurate more than 60% of the time. Bottom line – **These guys are guessing!**

> Journal of Investing, Summer 1997
> quoted by Swedroe, *The Only Guide to a Winning Investment Strategy You'll Ever Need*, p 90

What Wall Street and the financial media won't tell you is that the smart money has abandoned active management stock picking and market timing. Developed by Nobel Prize winning academics and now utilized by more than half of the institutional money, Modern Portfolio Theory is not well known to the general public.

"Most investors, both institutional and individual, will find that the best way to own common stocks is through an index fund that charges minimal fees. Those following this path are sure to beat the results (after fees and expenses) delivered by the great majority of investment professionals"

Warren Buffet, Feb 1977,
Letter to Shareholders

"The deterioration of performance by professionals is getting worse. But the public thinks they are doing great because the average fund is up...But, they'd be better off in an index fund"

Peter Lynch

"Hopelessly unpopular with investment managers and with most clients, the uninspiring, dull 'market portfolio' (or 'index fund') is seldom given anything like the respect it deserves. Plodding along in its unimaginative, inexpensive 'no-brainer' way, this 'plain Jane' form of investing will, over time, achieve better results than most professional investment managers."

Charles Ellis, *The Loser's Game*, p 17

Don't sell a simple index fund strategy short.

Part Three

Modern Investing

Chapter 18
Modern Portfolio Theory

Abstract - Modern Portfolio Theory (MPT) has changed the investment landscape. MPT began with the insight of Harry Markowitz in 1952 that portfolio diversification can reduce portfolio volatility (risk) and increase its return, if the assets in the portfolio have low correlation. MPT has even changed the legal definition of prudence in its impact on the rewriting of the Prudent Investor Rule (now law in most states).

The landmark event in the development of modern portfolio theory was the discovery by Harry Markowitz that diversification – combining assets with low correlation in a portfolio – can **reduce overall risk and increase the portfolio's return**.

His findings were published as *Portfolio Selection* in the Journal of Finance, March 1952 (p 77-91). Mean Variance Optimization, the process of analyzing alternative combinations of portfolio assets, with varying returns, risks and correlations, is the statistical innovation that Markowitz brought to investment science. Harry Markowitz, William Sharpe and Merton Miller were awarded the Nobel Prize in Economic Sciences in 1990 for their work in Modern Portfolio Theory.

The bad news is that while Modern Portfolio Theory is practiced by nearly all large institutional investors, it remains unknown to most individual investors because most retail investment houses have not found a way to capitalize on its simple buy and hold diversification tenets. Some notable exceptions are Vanguard (the index fund powerhouse), Schwab (with its core indexing strategies) and Merrill Lynch (with their sector diversified portfolios).

Modern Portfolio Theory has changed the very definition of prudence. In 1990, in response to the overwhelming body of evidence about the unsatisfactory performance of active managers and the benefits of passive asset class investing, the American Law Institute rewrote the Prudent Investor Rule. It has been made into law in most states. It is the law that governs the activities of financial managers.

Modern Portfolio Theory and the Prudent Investor Rule:

> *"Economic evidence shows that, from a typical investment perspective, the major capital markets of this country are **highly efficient**, in the sense that available information is rapidly digested and reflected in the market prices of securities.*
> *As a result, fiduciaries and other investors are confronted with **potent evidence that the application of expertise, investigation and diligence in efforts to 'beat the market'** in these publicly traded securities ordinarily **promises little or no payoff**, or even a **negative payoff** after taking account of research and transaction costs. Empirical research supporting the theory of efficient markets reveals that in such markets skilled professionals have **rarely** been able to identify under-priced securities (that is, to **out guess** the market with respect to future return) with any regularity. In fact, evidence shows that there is **little correlation** between fund managers' earlier successes and their ability to produce above-market returns in subsequent periods."*

> Reporter's Notes, p 75, The American Law Institute, *Restatement of the Law, Trust, Prudent Investor Rule*, 1992 (emphasis mine)

That is a pretty strong condemnation of active management – and an equally strong recommendation for Modern Portfolio Theory.

Chapter 19
Investment Statistics Basics

Abstract -   A little bit of statistics (the textbook stuff used by statisticians) is necessary to understand modern portfolio theory. The basics include standard deviation (as a measure of volatility – risk), regression to the mean, and normal distribution (bell-curve).

Stock market returns are generally quite random, falling both above and below zero and their averages, but with a very important upward bias. Over a long period of time, returns in a market or a part of a market remain fairly consistent. Periods of over- and under-trend performance are often followed by **regression to the mean**. Regression to the mean is a powerful reality in both nature and in investing. It is a technical term of probability and statistics. It means that, left to themselves, things tend to return to normal. The everyday expressions, "things will even out" and "the law of averages" both point at regression to the mean. Since average returns from asset classes tend to be very stable over long periods of time; you should expect periods of higher or lower than average performance to be followed by regression to the mean.

Returns fall around the average in a generally **normal distribution**, the familiar **bell-shaped frequency curve**. Returns fall both above and below the average, with so many more occurrences near the average that the curve bulges up into its bell-shape. The magnitude of the deviations away from the average is descriptive of the risk associated with the investment, and investment managers use the concept of **standard deviation** (a statistical term) to measure it.

The standard deviation tells how far above and below average returns are likely to be over time:

Returns will be within **One Standard Deviation** of average (either above or below) **68.26%** of the time (7 out of 10 years).

Returns will be within **Two Standard Deviations** of average (either above or below) **95.44%** of the time (19 out of 20 years).

Returns will be within **Three Standard Deviations** of average (either above or below) **99.75%** of the time (199 out of 200 years).

This measure of **volatility** informs us about how often things can, and will, get very weird. A return (or loss) two standard deviations from average is pretty weird, but count on it happening one in twenty years. Three standard deviations almost never happens, but don't count on never. It can, and will, happen about every 200 years (probably not in your lifetime, but who knows, it could happen).

The important knowledge for investors is that assets that have done very poorly in the recent past are likely to do better in the future. And conversely, assets that have done very well in the recent past are more likely to do poorly in the future. Significant deviations from long term historical averages will likely be "corrected" by regression to the mean (average). Every investor should be familiar with the concepts of normal distribution, standard deviation and regression to the mean. Ask your financial advisor to explain. If your advisor is not familiar with standard deviation, he (or she) is probably not familiar with modern portfolio theory.

Return and **Volatility** (Standard Deviation) together form the foundation of investment statistical analysis.

A diagram of the actual frequency of the returns of the S&P 500 is remarkably close to the normal distribution predicted by a 20% standard deviation around a 12% average return. The main difference is some 'skew' to the positive side. This "skew" to the positive reflects the growth of the economy as a whole.

The diagram below graphs the number of years with returns within one, two and three standard deviations of average.

FIGURE 19.1   S&P 500 NEAR NORMAL DISTRIBUTION
80 YEARS PERFORMANCE   1926 to 2006

Average return   12.3%
Standard Deviation   20.2%

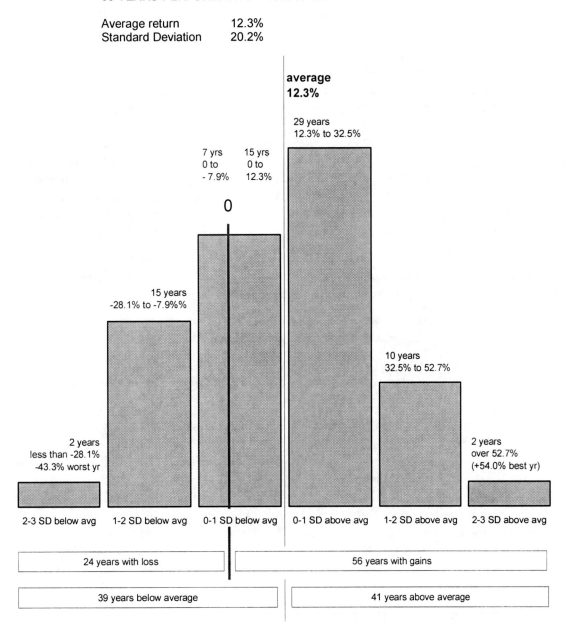

This is an attractive investment. Skewed towards gains, relatively good returns. The only problem: the returns are not consistent year to year. The example in the following chapter will help you understand the importance of decreasing volatility.

Chapter 20

The Benefits of Low Correlation and Reduced Volatility

Modern Portfolio Theory in a Nutshell

Abstract - Low correlation between investment asset classes reduces volatility and reduced volatility causes an increase in the annualized average return (even when the average rate of return is unchanged). Small reductions in volatility compound into significantly increased total returns over time. Percentage returns can be either average (arithmetic mean) or annualized (geometric mean); and expressed as either nominal or real (inflation adjusted) return.

First, a little about the mathematics of percentage returns. It is important to understand what kind of percentage return is under discussion. Generally, it will be either **average** return (the arithmetic mean) or **annualized** return (the geometric mean, sometimes called the compound return). Annualized return is sometimes called actual return. For now, just realize that the annualized return is always less than the average return in the investment world because returns vary from year to year; and this variability reduces the actual growth of the investment.

In addition, returns are often measured against inflation; creating two more flavors of returns: **nominal** returns and **real** (inflation adjusted) returns. To compare the returns of alternative investments, you must be sure you are talking about apples and apples.

Harry Markowitz discovered that you can increase returns over time, by reducing portfolio volatility, even when the average rate of return remains unchanged. Correlation was key.

If two assets move in exact tandem, they have a correlation of +1; if they moved in exactly opposite manner, their correlation would be –1. A portfolio benefits from the addition of assets with less than +1 correlation (assets that don't move in tandem).

My favorite example comes from Burton Malkiel and involves an island economy with two businesses. One is a resort that does well when it is sunny. The second is an umbrella maker that does well when it rains. The island has a weird climate. It rains half the years, and the sun shines the other half. Each business makes a profit of 50% when it does well and loses 25% when it does badly. Therefore they both have an average return of 12.5% (plus 50% minus 25% divided by 2); with an annual variation of 37.50% (either above or below the 12.50% average). If you only own one of the businesses you are stuck with the alternating gains and losses, but you could invest half of your money in each of the two businesses and level out your returns giving you a 12.5% every year. If you rebalanced the total investment to one half in each company at the end of every year, returns would be:

TABLE 20.1   ISLAND ECONOMY INVESTMENTS

	A Owning only the resort co.	B Owning only the umbrella co.	A+B Owning both companies together
Average Annual (arithmetic) Return	12.50%	12.50%	12.50%
Volatility (Deviation)	37.50%	37.50%	0%
Annualized Average (geometric) Return	6.07%	6.07%	12.50%
Value of $1,000 (20 yrs)	$3,247	$3,247	$10,545

FIGURE 20.2   ISLAND ECONOMY INVESTMENTS

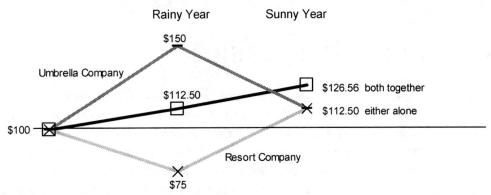

Think about how good the Umbrella Company investor feels after the first year (and how bad the Resort Company investor feels). The guy that bought both probably feels ok (but not all that good because he has to listen to the boasting of the Umbrella Company investor). In fact the guy that bought both is probably the quiet guy with not much to say about his investments around the water cooler (but in the end he has twice the return of the other two investors).

The **annualized rate of return** is not the same as the average annual rate of return because of the impact of volatility. In examples A & B, the good and bad years alternate. A $100 investment either grows to $150 in the first year then shrinks to **$112.50** at the end of the second year; or visa versa, shrinks to $75 the first year and then grows to **$112.50** at the end of the second year. In example C, the 12.50% rate of return is constant and the $100 grows to $112.50 at the end of the first year and then to **$126.56** at the end of the second year. This difference after two years (more than twice the total return) really adds up after 20 years.

The extreme volatility in the resort co./umbrella co. example is seldom approached in the real world. In the real world there are no perfectly negatively correlated assets. Assets with a correlation of +0.3 or higher are considered positively correlated. A correlation of -0.3 or less is considered negative correlation. There are many assets with poor or even mildly negative correlations that will improve your portfolio's performance.

The following example further illustrates the negative impact of volatility on an otherwise reasonable rate of return. In the example each portfolio has the same average annual rate of return of 12% (approximately the 80 year average of the S&P 500). The range of standard deviations, from 30% for the speculator (gambler) to 10% for a Modern Portfolio Theory portfolio, is a good representation of the limits that you should expect. The final column shows the return of an utterly imaginary portfolio with zero volatility (the high limit of performance). Notice especially, the improvement in the annualized average return of the modern portfolio over the S&P 500 that results from the reduction in volatility. This improvement is available to you if you invest in a modern portfolio. Chapters 28 to 33 show you how.

TABLE 20.3   PORTFOLIO VOLATILITY AND RETURNS

	Speculator/ Gambler		S&P 500 75 yr avg		Modern Portfolio	Zero Volatility
Average Annual Return	12.00%	12.00%	12.00%	12.00%	12.00%	12.00%
Volatility (Std Deviation)	30.00%	25.00%	20.00%	15.00%	10.00%	0.00%
Annualized Average Return	8.05%	9.27%	10.26%	11.04%	11.57%	12.00%
Value of $1,000 (20 yrs)	$4,700	$5,890	$7,060	$8,110	$8,940	$9,650

Reducing volatility is the heart of risk management; reducing risk and improving returns. The good news is that combining risky (high return) assets can reduce risk and increase return! Reducing your risk is the key to increasing returns.

Chapter 21
Investment Risk Basics

Abstract -   There are three kinds of investment risk – individual stock risk, stock group risk and market risk. The first two have no return and should be eliminated through diversification. The remaining market risk is almost entirely a short-term phenomenon. Reducing volatility (most easily measured by standard deviation) will not only reduce your risk; but will also increase your return at the same time. The simplest measure of risk management success is standard deviation.

There are three kinds of investment risk.

Individual Stock Risk (called specific risk in academia) is the risk associated with any individual company or stock. Having all of your retirement nestegg invested in Enron or GM or any other single stock, is a lot of individual stock risk. Individual stock risk can be virtually eliminated by diversification (most simply by purchasing a broad market index fund).

Stock Group Risk (called extra market risk in academia) is the risk associated with a market sector or business sector. Having all your retirement nestegg invested in energy companies or automotive companies is a lot of stock group risk. Stock group risk can also be virtually eliminated by diversification (again most simply by purchasing a broad market index fund).

Market Risk (called systematic risk in academia) must be managed because it cannot be eliminated. Market risk can be managed by reducing portfolio volatility.

> *"In an efficient market no incremental reward can or will be earned over the market rate of return by taking either more individual stock risk or more stock group risk"*
>
> Charles Ellis, *The Loser's Game*, p 47

Overwhelming evidence confirms that the market is efficient, and that active management strategies (stock picking and market timing) don't work. Much financial media energy (and anecdotal personal success stories from friends and associates) is focused on convincing us that this stuff can be "picked." It can't. There is no **long-term** reward for individual stock risk or stock group risk, both are gambling – period!

The use of broad market index funds eliminates individual stock and stock group risk. Diversification into a number of poorly correlated broad market level index funds can reduce risk (standard deviation) and increase return at the same time.

Because volatility (as we saw in the last chapter) robs your portfolio of long-term returns, reducing volatility (standard deviation) should be a primary goal of investment and portfolio management. This is a concept of fundamental importance to investors. Modern Portfolio Theory allows you to design portfolios that reduce volatility (risk) and increase returns. Standard deviation is the simplest, and most easily available measure of portfolio risk.

Time changes everything. The risk of a bad result decreases dramatically with time. The longer your time horizon, the more likely you are to achieve something closer to the "average" return of your portfolio. The short run is a crap shoot.

> *"The stock market is fascinating and very deceptive in the short run. In the very long run, the market is almost boringly reliable"*
>
> Charles Ellis, *The Loser's Game*, p 15

Chapter 22
Stock Market Return Basics

Abstract - Returns for the last 30 years have been very high by some historical standards. Rational investors should not plan on these returns continuing into the future. The expected equity premium (the additional return from stocks over relatively risk free gov't bonds) has been the subject of intense debate in the academic and investment communities. Awareness of actual returns and equity premium of the long-term is critical to understanding the debate. Historical and reasonable future returns are outlined.

Navigation Tip

This is a very difficult chapter – a lot of numbers and arcane concepts. For now, if you don't want to wade through all of it, simply look at the concluding tables (page 55) and come back to the rest of the chapter later. You need to know the kind of arguments that are being made in the academic and investment communities.

It may seem like common knowledge that stocks have historically had higher returns than bonds. In fact, in the 1800's the common knowledge held that stocks were for speculators and insiders. Conservative investors preferred bonds. The first credible study of long-term returns that demonstrated that stocks had higher returns than bonds was *Common Stocks as Long-Term Investments* by Edgar Lawrence Smith (1926). Looking at data from 1901 to 1922, his book, coming at the beginning of the roaring twenties bull market, was widely read (and for a few years very influential) in both academic and investment circles. The crash of 1929 put stocks back in the doghouse.

In 1964 Fisher and Lorie published a study of *Rates of Return on Investment in Common Stocks* in the Journal of Business (January 1964). Their study was based on the first computerized database of stock prices recently completed by the University of Chicago's Center for Research in Security Prices (CRSP, pronounced "crisp"). They reported the return on common stocks from 1926 to 1964 to be 9.1% (far more than bonds or any other investment over this period).

Two important studies since the above have had special influence on the expectations of the investment community regarding stock market returns. The first was *Stocks, Bonds, Bills and Inflation: Year-by-Year Historical Returns 1926-1974*, by Roger Ibbotson and Rex Sinquefield. This book was published in the middle of the worst bear market since the great depression. Their data has been revised annually since then and has had substantial influence regarding investors' expectations.

TABLE 22.1   AVERAGE RETURNS of STOCKS, BONDS, BILLS and INFLATION

	Inflation	Avg Return Large Stocks	Average Real Return Large Stocks	Annualized Real Return Large Stocks
1926 to 1974 (first edition)	2.3%	10.8%	8.5%	5.9%
1926 to 1999 (market peak)	3.2%	13.3%	11.3%	8.0%
1926 to 2006	3.1%	12.3%	9.2%	7.1%

Year after year, the Ibbotson yearbook has reported the average returns since 1926 and the expectation of these high returns has become "common knowledge" in the investment community. The 8.5% to 9.2% (peaking at 11.3% in 1999) average real return of stocks has profoundly influenced the expectations of investors.

The second book having special influence is *Stocks for the Long Run* by Jeremy Siegel (2002). The constancy of real annualized stock market returns in his data has caused 6.7% (or 6.6% to 7.0%) to be termed "Seigel's Constant." Siegel's 6.7% and Ibbotson's 7.1% are substantially in agreement regarding real annualized returns from 1926 to 2006.

TABLE 22.2   **ANNUALIZED REAL STOCK MARKET RETURNS**

		Real Annualized Returns		
		Stock Market	Bonds	Equity Premium
1802 to 1870	transition from agrarian to industrial	7.0%	4.8%	2.2%
1871 to 1925	US became a political & economic superpower	6.6%	3.7%	2.9%
1926 to 2005	stock market crash, great depression & post war	6.7%	2.3%	4.4%
1946 to 2005	post world war II period	6.8%	1.5%	5.3%

Jeremy Siegel, 2005, presented at Wharton School SIA Annual Meeting

While the real returns of the stock market have been remarkably consistent over the whole period, bond returns and the equity premium (the excess return of stocks over bonds) have not been consistent (except in their movement direction). The equity premium has been rising throughout the period. The real return of bonds has been falling. The falling bond return relates to the decreasing risk of the US Treasury which was an emerging market democracy at the beginning of the series and the measure of risk-free investment at the end. The rising equity premium is a puzzle that has been the subject of intense debate in both academia and the investment community; with most arguing for far lower equity premium in the future. Those arguing for a low forward looking equity premium typically do so by deconstructing equity returns into current dividend yield and expected growth.

Gordon Formula now a Puzzle

With the Gordon Constant Growth Dividend Discount Model (a widely used model for predicting long-term stock value) you can project the future value of a stock (or a whole market) and therefore the forward looking equity premium. In the Gordon formula, price equals dividend yield plus future dividend growth. The dividend discount model assumes that all companies eventually go bankrupt; that the only value of a company is its dividends (the present value of all future dividends). Therefore long-term market return = dividend yield + dividend growth rate (the dividend growth rate is roughly equal to the GNP growth rate).

TABLE 22.3   **HISTORICAL DIVIDEND YIELD and GNP GROWTH RATE with GORDON FORMULA ESTIMATED FUTURE RETURNS and P/E RATIOS**

	Dividend Yield	Real GNP Growth Rate	Gordon formula return	Actual period realized	Price/Earnings P/E (10 year) Ratio
1926 to 1954	5.49%	3.85%	9.34%	9.56%	13.88
1955 to 1991	3.79%	3.42%	7.21%	10.99%	15.23
1992 to 2006	1.95%	3.21%	5.16%	10.44%	27.95
1926 to 2006	4.06%	3.54%	7.60%	10.37%	16.97

The Gordon Formula return for the early period (1926-1954) data produces long-term returns for the market almost exactly equal to the realized return. The realized returns from the later periods vary much more dramatically from the Gordon formula. This disparity is the equity premium puzzle. **Either the standard theory is wrong, or we should expect much lower returns in the future.** The Gordon Formula return for the period from the 1992-2006 is 5.16% (far lower than historical returns). With bonds returning about 4.5% that leaves only a 0.6% equity premium. Hard to believe. The Gordon Formula ignores the value of a company's capital assets – maybe they are important.

P/E Ratio has Shifted (Permanently?)

The upward shift in Price/Earnings (P/E) ratio now into the mid 20's, over these periods is often cited as a reason to expect future regression to a mean average near 14.0 to 17.0. There are many factors that suggest this regression will **not** occur (that P/E ratios will remain at the new higher level permanently). These include: the new "common knowledge" that stocks are superior long-term; a more stable economy (a major reduction in economic volatility); dramatically lower transaction costs (both commissions and bid-ask-spread); the favorable tax treatment for equities (lower cap gain and dividend tax and rates); and a shift from dividend payout toward stock repurchase and reinvestment (this shift adds yield for existing stockholders of from 0.5% to 1%).

There are a number of credible academic studies that point toward permanent structural shifts in the P/E ratio around 1954 and 1991. Investors are now willing to pay more for stocks (and the underlying earnings and dividends) than they were before. Price (P) is permanently higher; Earnings (E) have grown, but only in line with GDP growth. Over the last 50 years, the increase in price (relative to earnings) has added a substantial "capital gain return" to stocks (in addition to the Gordon Formula return from dividends and growth). A move from a P/E of 15 to a P/E of 25 involves a 66.67% capital gain (10 increase divided by 15 initial value). A reversion to the old 15 P/E would involve a 40% capital loss (10 decrease divided by 25 initial value).

But even if the P/E shift is permanent, we should expect lower earnings going forward. Dividend yield is now just under 2% having been just over 4% over the 20th century. Total returns going forward are likely to be about this much (the 2% difference) below historical averages.

In 2002, a new landmark study joined the other very influential books above: *The Triumph of the Optimists: 101 Years of Global Investment Returns,* Elroy Dimson, Paul Marsh and Mike Staunton (2002). This new book provides information from the US and 16 countries around the world for the entire 20th century (1900-2000).

Dimson, Marsh and Staunton argue that the US has been remarkably successful in the last century and that it would be dangerous for investors to extrapolate the last US century into the future. They present slightly lower returns than Ibbotson and Siegel, but remain in substantial agreement regarding the general level of returns.

TABLE 22.4   **TRUMPH OF THE OPTIMISTS DATA COMPARISON**

	Average Real Return Large Stocks	Annualized Real Return Large Stocks	Annualized Real Return Long-Term Bonds	Historical Equity Premium
Ibbotson (1926-2001)	9.2%	7.4%	2.0%	5.4%
Siegel (1926-2001)	8.9%	6.9%	2.2%	4.7%
Dimson Marsh Staunton (1900-2000)	8.7%	6.7%	1.6%	5.1%

A Wide Range of Predictions

Estimates of the forward-looking equity premium range from the historical past premium to zero (or even less). Influential personalities argue for all possible outcomes. And since the future is essentially unknowable, we cannot be certain who is right. All we know today is that there is a lot of debate. A representative group is outlined in the following table. As you can see below, Dimson, Marsh and Staunton are more pessimistic than Ibbotson, but more optimistic than Siegel and many others.

TABLE 22.5 **RANGE of FUTURE PREDICTED EQUITY PREMIUM**
Based on Large Cap Stocks over Long-Term Govt Bonds

	Arithmetic Mean	Geometric Mean
Historical Average (1926-2006)	6.5%	5.0%
Ibbotson (2003, 2005)[1]	**5.9%**	**4.0%**
Dimson, Marsh, Staunton (2006)[2]	**4.5 – 5.0%**	**3.0 - 3.5%**
Siegel (2005)[3]	**4.0%**	**3.0%**
Swedroe (2003)[4]	3.8%	
Campbell (2001)[5]	3.0 – 4.0%	1.5 – 2.5%
Shoven (2001)[5]	2.5 – 3.5%	
Diamond (2001)[5]	1.0 – 1.5%	
Arnott & Bernstein (2002)[6]	zero	
Arnott & Ryan (2001)[7]	-1% (negative)	

1 Roger G. Ibbotson and Peter Chen
   Long-Run Stock Returns: Participating in the Real Economy
   Financial Analysts Journal, January/February 2003

2 Elroy Dimson, Paul Marsh and Mike Staunton
   The Worldwide Equity Premium: A Smaller Puzzle
   London Business School, online article revised 11 April 2006

3 Presentation by Jeremy J. Siegel at The Wharton School
   Bull vs Bear Debate
   SIA Annual Meeting, November 10, 2005

4 Buckingham Asset Management, Larry Swedroe (editor)
   The Educated Investor, May 2003

5 John Y. Campbell, Peter A. Diamond and John B. Shoven,
   Estimating the Real Rate of Return on Stocks Over the Long Term, Presented to the Social Security Advisory Board, Aug 2001

6 Robert D. Arnott and Peter L. Bernstein
   What Risk Premium is "Normal,"
   Financial Analysts Journal, March/April 2002

7 Robert D. Arnott and Ronald J. Ryan
   The Death of the Risk Premium
   The Journal of Portfolio Management, Spring 2001

I am inclined to give the Ibbotson-DMS-Siegel range from 4% to 6% (arithmetic) more weight. Not that any of the more pessimistic experts are lightweights by any means. I am using a 5% (arithmetic) future equity premium for my personal planning purposes.

Vanguard recently published a nine part summary of its investment philosophy. In part nine Vanguard says: *"We believe ... an investor should not expect future long-term returns to be significantly higher or lower than long-term historical returns for various asset classes and subclasses. ...As with stock returns as a whole, it is our view that there is no compelling reason to assume that future equity risk premiums will be significantly different from past premiums over long periods."*

Conclusions

Over any long-term period, stocks have done better than bonds and are likely to continue to do better under almost all outlooks. How much better is clearly a matter of some debate.

Past returns over the last 15, 32 and 80 years are shown in the following table.

TABLE 22.6   HISTORICAL INVESTMENT RETURNS

	Real Return (arithmetic)	Real Return (annualized)	Total Return	Std Dev
80 years from 1926 to 2006				
Inflation			3.1%	4.3%
Treasury Bills	0.6%	0.5%	3.8%	3.1%
Intermediate Term Govt Bonds	2.4%	2.1%	5.5%	5.7%
Long-Term Govt Bonds	2.7%	2.1%	5.8%	9.2%
Stocks **(S&P 500)**	9.2%	7.1%	12.3%	20.1%
Equity Premium (over long-term bond)	6.5%			
32 years from 1975 to 2006				
Inflation			4.4%	3.0%
Treasury Bills	1.6%	1.6%	6.0%	3.1%
Intermediate Term Govt Bonds	4.1%	3.8%	8.5%	6.8%
Long-Term Govt Bonds	5.5%	4.7%	9.9%	12.0%
Stocks **(S&P 500)**	10.2%	9.0%	14.6%	15.7%
Equity Premium (over long-term bond)	4.7%			
15 years from 1992 to 2006				
Inflation			2.6%	0.7%
Treasury Bills	1.1%	1.1%	3.8%	1.6%
Intermediate Term Govt Bonds	3.8%	3.6%	6.4%	6.0%
Long-Term Govt Bonds	6.2%	5.6%	8.8%	11.1%
Stocks **(S&P 500)**	9.3%	7.9%	12.0%	17.4%
Equity Premium (over long-term bond)	3.1%			

Source: DFA, Ibbotson

Dimson, Marsh and Staunton indicate that the short term (5, 10 to 30 years) while not useful in estimating future returns, is useful regarding forecasts of future volatility. They agree with a large number of other scholars and investment analysts that overall market volatility is decreasing. The lower volatility of the second half of the 20th century (16-18%, down from 20% over the whole century) is likely to be predictive of future market volatility.

TABLE 22.7   PROJECTED FUTURE RETURNS

	Real Return (arithmetic)	Real Return (annualized)	Total Return (nominal)	Std Dev
Assumed Future Equity Premium	5.0%			
Inflation			3.0%	3.0%
Treasury Bills	0.5%	0.5%	3.5%	3.0%
Intermediate Term Govt Bonds	1.7%	1.5%	4.7%	6.0%
Long Term Govt Bonds	2.0%	1.8%	5.0%	13.0%
Stocks **(S&P 500)**	7.0%	6.3%	10.0%	17.0%

If you are not comfortable with a 5.0% equity premium projection, you can reduce equity returns further.

Several asset classes have been identified by research that have higher returns than the S&P 500 (large cap stocks) or the market as a whole.

Chapter 23

Asset Class Research
Small Cap and Value Stock Investing
The Three Factor Model

Abstract - Several asset classes have been identified by research that have higher returns than the market as a whole. The benefit to your portfolio from adding these is compounded because they not only increase average return, but also reduce volatility (risk) since they tend to be poorly correlated with the market as whole (and each other). This is really big news! Two broad asset classes in particular – small cap and value – have been identified as providing higher return than the market as a whole.

Based on the Center for Research in Securities Pricing (CRSP) data, several capitalization based asset classes have been the focus of modern portfolio theory research. CRSP divides the entire equities market into ten deciles based on the market capitalization of the New York Stock Exchange. This methodology forms the basis for much more scientific analysis of asset class returns. CRSP deciles allow for precise definitions of market capitalization (large cap, small cap and micro cap).

TABLE 23.1   CRSP DECILES   CAPITALIZATION and NUMBER OF COMPANIES

Decile	Size (millions)	NYSE	AMEX	NASDAQ	TOTAL
1	$511,391	172	5	80	257
2	10,486	172	3	81	256
3	4,428	172	5	136	313
4	2,237	172	5	166	343
5	1,387	172	5	217	394
6	889	172	11	254	437
7	534	172	15	251	438
8	353	172	32	400	604
9	198	172	73	551	796
10	95	172	412	1,399	1,983
Totals		1,720	566	3,535	5,821

The S&P 500 is roughly coterminous with deciles 1 & 2. The Russell 2000 Small Cap Index covers approximately deciles 5-8. Deciles 9 & 10 are micro cap. The Wilshire 5000 covers the whole market (it used to be closer to 5000 stocks, now it's more). CRSP uses a similar decile system to analyze book-to-market value, creating in effect a 10 x 10 style box. This is a substantial improvement over the more anecdotal Morningstar style boxes, which has only 9 boxes of texture to define the market.

While the Morningstar style boxes are an important innovation, they provide limited and sometimes misleading information. For instance, both a Russell 2000 and a CRSP 9-10 fund would be called "small cap" in the Morningstar system. The micro cap stocks, and their return premium, are obscured. Regarding value, most retail value funds hold stocks in the bottom half of book-to-market value that dilutes the lowest deciles of value. DFA value funds, based on

CRSP size and value deciles, hold stocks only in the bottom 10% of value for large cap stocks and the bottom 25% for small cap stocks. All small is not the same; all value is not the same.

FIGURE 23.2   CRSP DECILES and MORNINGSTAR STYLE BOXES

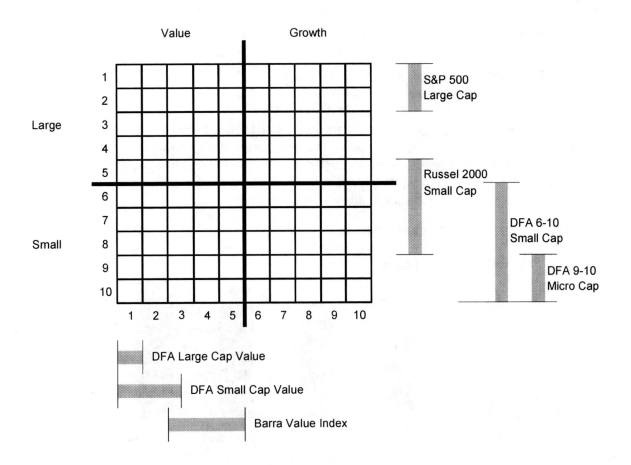

CRSP Deciles

Morningstar Style Boxes

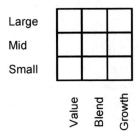

The original research on the size effect was performed by Rolf Banz. He found in 1981 that returns increase with decreases in size as measured by market capitalization.

Rolf Banz, *The Relationship Between Return and Market Value of Common Stocks*, Journal of Financial Economics, Mar 1981, p 3-18

A decade of debate followed in the academic and investment communities. The influential work of Eugene Fama and Kenneth French researching the impact of market, size and value exposure on portfolio returns was published in *The Cross Section of Expected Stock Returns*, Journal of Finance, June 1992, (p 427-465). The Fama French 3-Factor Model can be summarized as follows:

Equity Premium   Stocks have higher expected return than bonds

Size Premium   Small company stocks have higher expected returns than large company stocks

Value Premium   Lower-priced "value" stocks have higher expected return than higher-priced "growth" stocks

Their findings can be seen graphically in the following chart. The difference between bonds and the S&P 500 represents the equity premium or exposure to the stock market (an overwhelming influence on portfolio return). Exposure to small company and value stocks can add some additional return. The historical equity premium is visible (7.13% less 2.15% = 4.98%); the historical size and value premiums are similarly visible.

FIGURE 23.3   **ASSET CLASS RETURNS**

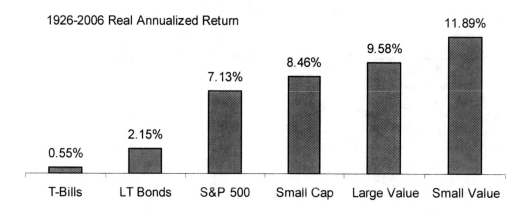

The small cap premium can be seen in two comparisons: large cap to small cap (8.46% less 7.13% = 1.33%) and small value to large value (11.89% less 9.58% = 2.31%). The value premium can be seen in two similar comparisons: large value to large cap (9.58% less 7.13% = 2.45%) and small value to small cap (11.89% less 8.46% = 3.43%).

Value investing involves companies that are not currently doing well. These "distressed" companies are low priced, those trading closest to their "liquidation" value. They are called high book-to-market value companies (but it is really their market value that is low; book value is high only relative to the low market value). Companies with a high book-to-market value are risky companies. It turns out that these **risky** companies make **great** investments (while great companies may not) – counterintuitive!

Michele Clayman studied and compared excellent and unexcellent companies in her research of value investing. She published *In search of Excellence: The Investor's Viewpoint*, Financial Analysts Journal, June 1987, p 63; and *Excellence Revisited*, Financial Analysts Journal, May-June 1994, p 61-65. She found that, as investments, "unexcellent" companies significantly outperformed "excellent" companies. This does not mean that "unexcellent" companies outperformed "excellent" companies, as companies; they did not. But "unexcellent" companies were better investments. For the period 1981-1985 she found the following:

TABLE 23.4   UNEXCELLENT AND EXCELLENT COMPANIES

	Unexcellent Companies	Excellent Companies
Asset Growth	5.93%	21.78%
Equity Growth	3.76%	18.43%
Return on Total Capital	4.88%	16.04%
Return on Equity	7.09%	19.05%
Return on Sales	2.49%	8.62%
Return on $100 Investment	$297.50	$181.60

Unexcellent companies – great investments!

Warren Buffet is perhaps the most famous value investor in the world.

> *"The best available data would indicate that a strong tilt to value and a higher representation of small company stocks in equity portfolios will handsomely reward long-term investors"*

> Frank Armstrong, Investment Advisor

There have been many nay-sayers about the small cap effect in recent years. The recent superior performance of large cap stocks from 1995 to 1998 with the S&P 500 averaging over 30% return and small caps only about 15% has fueled some of the discussion. Research has documented that the size effect weakened from 1982 to 2001 but since then has been very strong.

Dimson, Marsh and Staunton in the *Triumph of the Optimists* put forward the idea that the size premium (small cap over large cap) had even reversed. They presented compelling data from the United States, United Kingdom and around the world (from the 20th century) showing that once the size premium was discovered in a market it was exploited for a few honeymoon years and then it disappeared. John Bogle (the founder of Vanguard) has expressed similar doubts about size and value investing; recommending Total Stock Market Index investing.

The recent bear market (2000 to 2002) and subsequent recovery (2003 through 2006) indicate the reports of the death of the size premium were greatly exaggerated. See Table 23.4 below. In this table you can see that investment in both small cap and value stocks paid off handsomely in the bear market (with lower losses) and then in the recovery (with clearly superior gains).

In every period, except the 90's bull market, small cap and value outperformed large cap stocks (by significant margins). And even in the 90's bull market, small cap and value did very well; just not as well as the spectacular performance of the S&P 500 in that period.

TABLE 23.5 **HISTORICAL INVESTMENT RETURNS**

Legend: 7.1% real annualized return
12.3 (20.1) average nominal return (standard deviation in parentheses)

	1926 to 2006	1975 to 2006	90's Bull Market 1992 to 1999	Bear Market 2000 to 2002	Recovery 2003 to 2006
Inflation	0.0%	0.0%	0.0%	0.0%	0.0%
	3.1 (4.3)	4.4 (3.9)	2.5 (0.6)	2.4 (0.9)	3.1 (0.9)
Treasury Bills	0.6%	1.6%	2.0%	1.3%	-0.8%
	3.8 (3.1)	6.0 (3.1)	4.5 (1.0)	3.8 (2.1)	2.3 (1.5)
Intermediate Govt Bonds	2.1%	3.8%	3.3%	8.4%	0.7%
	5.5 (5.7)	8.5 (6.8)	6.0 (7.1)	10.9 (5.0)	3.8 (1.7)
Long-Term Govt Bonds	2.1%	4.7%	5.3%	11.7%	1.9%
	5.8 (9.2)	9.9 (12.0)	8.7 (14.0)	14.3 (9.4)	5.0 (3.6)
Large Cap Stocks (S&P 500)	7.1%	9.2%	17.1%	-17.0%	11.6%
	12.3 (20.1)	14.8 (15.9)	20.3 (12.9)	-14.4 (6.8)	15.0 (10.1)
Small Cap (deciles 6-10)	8.5%	12.7%	12.4%	-4.7%	18.4%
	15.9 (30.5)	18.7 (19.9)	15.6 (12.8)	-1.3 (16.2)	22.6 (19.0)
Micro Cap (deciles 9-10)	9.7%	14.0%	14.9%	-1.7%	20.5%
	18.8 (38.2)	20.3 (21.4)	18.1 (13.8)	2.0 (18.7)	25.4 (24.6)
Large Cap Value	9.6%	12.2%	14.9%	-3.3%	17.1%
	15.9 (26.3)	17.8 (16.2)	18.2 (13.7)	-0.3 (13.0)	20.5 (9.6)
Small Cap Value	11.9%	16.3%	14.8%	4.2%	24.1%
	19.3 (31.0)	22.1 (18.9)	18.2 (14.4)	7.5 (16.0)	28.6 (22.1)

Source: DFA, Ibbotson

Based on a 5.0% equity premium over long-term bonds, the following are projected future returns of these asset classes with a 1% to 2% size premium and a 2% value premium.

TABLE 23.6 **PROJECTED FUTURE RETURNS**

	Real Return (arithmetic)	Real Return (annualized)	Total Return (nominal)	Std Dev
Inflation			3.0%	3.0%
Treasury Bills	0.5%	0.5%	3.5%	3.0%
Intermediate Term Govt Bonds	1.7%	1.5%	4.7%	6.0%
Long Term Govt Bonds	2.0%	1.8%	5.0%	13.0%
Large Cap Stocks (S&P 500)	7.0%	6.3%	10.0%	17.0%
Small Cap (deciles 6-10)	8.0%	7.0%	11.0%	19.0%
Micro Cap (deciles 9-10)	9.0%	7.9%	12.0%	20.0%
Large Cap Value	9.0%	8.0%	12.0%	16.0%
Small Cap Value	11.0%	9.7%	14.0%	18.0%

In the next chapter we will look at the research on international stocks.

Chapter 24
International Investing

Abstract - The US outperformed the rest of the world in the 20th century. International small, value and emerging markets have outperformed the U.S. since 1970. U.S. growth is likely to be more moderate in the future while the rest of the world continues to grow strongly, especially in emerging markets. International equities should be included in a modern portfolio because of their good returns and low correlation to U.S. markets. Emerging markets have particularly low correlation.

Our knowledge of international equities markets is limited. Morgan Stanley Capital International (MSCI) has since 1970 calculated the returns from 23 developed countries in its widely used Europe, Australia and Far East (EAFE) foreign stock market index. This is essentially the S&P 500 for the rest of the world (including about 85% of non-U.S. world market capitalization). Emerging market data (for another 33 countries) dates from only 1988.

Dimson, Marsh and Staunton's *Triumph of the Optimists; 101 Years of Global Investment Returns* (2002) provided for the first time a look at the whole 20th century investment returns of the USA and 15 other countries around the world. While their database includes only 15 countries outside of the US, it is still quite remarkable in its breadth and depth. Their work stretched our knowledge of US investment returns as well back to the beginning of the century; where before we were generally limited to Ibbotson's data reaching only back to 1926.

At the start of the 21st century, the United States simply dominates the world equity markets with 46.1% of the total world market capitalization. The five largest capital markets (US, Japan, UK, France and Germany) account for 75% of the world's stock market. The 23 developed countries (adding Canada, Italy, the Netherlands, Switzerland, Hong Kong, Australia, Spain, Finland, Sweden, Belgium, Singapore, Denmark, Austria, Ireland, New Zealand, Norway and Portugal) account for about 92% of the world's markets. The next 33 emerging market countries are less than 8% of the world's markets.

It is very hard to expect the US economy and markets, with its GDP now growing at about 3.0% to outpace a world and emerging markets growing at 4.3% and 5.3%. The US is expected to grow faster than "Old Europe," but the rest of the world is expected to grow faster yet.

TABLE 24.1   POPULATION, GDP and GDP GROWTH

	Population (000)	GDP (000,000)	GDP per Capita	3 yr avg GDP Growth	Future GDP Growth Est
EAFE (Europe 16 Countries)	395,000	$11,539,000	$29,235	1.5%	2.4%
22 Developed Countries (excluding US)	591,000	17,773,000	30,071	2.0%	2.3%
23 Developed Countries (including US)	891,000	30,173,000	33,863	2.6%	2.3%
United States	300,000	12,400,000	41,333	3.6%	3.0%
23 Developed Countries + 33 Emerging	4,872,000	55,263,000	11,343	4.5%	3.8%
WORLD (all 216 countries)	6,252,000	60,630,000	9,697	4.4%	4.0%
WORLD (excluding US)	5,952,000	48,230,000	8,103	4.7%	4.3%
33 Emerging Market Countries	3,981,000	25,090,000	6,302	6.8%	5.3%

Source: CIA Country Factbook; OECD Economic Outlook

Choosing to invest only in the U.S. is choosing to forgo more than half of the investment opportunities in the world. A lot of them are outperforming the U.S. now, and are expected to continue growing.

In the US bull market in the 1990's, the US dollar gained about 25% against major world currencies (depressing international returns for US investors by about 2.5% per year). In the recent bear market, the dollar was very mixed against world currencies (with not much impact on US international investors). In the recovery from 2003 on, the dollar has lost 25% to 30% against major world currencies (inflating the gains of US international investors by about 8% per year). Many economists expect continuing weakness in the dollar which would be bullish for international investment by U.S. investors.

TABLE 24.2   HISTORICAL INVESTMENT RETURNS (IN USD)

Legend: 8.0%   real annualized return
          13.3 (20.2)   average nominal return (standard deviation in parentheses)

	20th Century 1900 to 2000	1975 to 2006	90's Bull Market 1992 to 1999	Bear Market 2000 to 2002	Recovery 2003 to 2006
United States	6.7% 11.8 (20.2)	9.0% 14.6 (15.7)	17.1% 20.3 (12.9)	-17.0% -14.4 (6.8)	11.6% 15.0 (10.1)
United Kingdom	5.8% 10.7 (20.0)	12.1% 18.8 (25.5)	12.0% 15.1 (11.8)	-16.0% -13.6 (1.9)	18.9% 22.4 (11.5)
World (except US)	5.2%	8.4% 14.7 (20.2)	8.8% 12.2 (14.4)	-19.1% -16.6 (4.1)	22.0% 25.5 (10.7)
International Large Cap		10.6% 17.0 (21.7)	7.9% 11.2 (13.4)	-19.0% -16.5 (3.8)	20.0% 23.5 (10.0)
International Small Cap		13.3% 20.6 (27.0)	0.5% 4.6 (19.1)	-7.1% -4.6 (6.1)	30.2% 34.1 (16.9)
International Large Cap Value		13.5% 19.9 (21.9)	9.1% 12.5 (15.8)	-10.6% -8.0 (7.6)	28.3% 32.0 (14.3)
International Small Cap Value		n/a	0.6% 4.4 (17.6)	-3.2% -0.6 (5.6)	34.1% 38.2 (19.4)
Emerging Markets		n/a	15.6% 21.7 (33.3)	-18.3% -15.1 (12.2)	33.5% 37.3 (15.3)
Annualized Currency Gain(Loss)			-2.5% +/-	0% +/-	+8% +/-

Source: DFA, Ibbotson, Dimson, Marsh and Staunton

At the beginning of the 20th century the UK dominated the world markets. Throughout the last century the UK was in comparative decline. But its returns trailed the US by only a little as you can see in table 24.2 above. UK returns last century were a little higher than the world average (without the US). Dimson, Marsh and Staunton point toward the UK experience last century as reasonable for the US to expect this century. The US should not expect to continue to outperform the world, but it should continue to do very well.

The rest of the world is reasonably expected to continue to grow. And growth is expected to be especially strong in emerging markets.

TABLE 24.3   PROJECTED FUTURE RETURNS

	Real Return (arithmetic)	Real Return (annualized)	Total Return (nominal)	Std Dev
Inflation			3.0%	3.0%
US Large Cap	7.0%	6.3%	10.0%	17.0%
US Small Cap	8.0%	7.0%	11.0%	19.0%
US Micro Cap	9.0%	7.9%	12.0%	20.0%
US Large Cap Value	9.0%	8.0%	12.0%	16.0%
US Small Cap Value	11.0%	9.7%	14.0%	18.0%
International Large Cap	8.0%	7.0%	11.0%	17.5%
International Small Cap	9.0%	8.0%	12.0%	19.5%
International Large Cap Value	10.0%	8.8%	13.0%	16.5%
International Small Cap Value	12.0%	10.6%	15.0%	22.5%
Emerging Markets	13.0%	11.5%	16.0%	27.5%

"Just as investors a decade ago were overly optimistic about foreign diversification, investors today are overly pessimistic about it. Foreign stocks belong in every portfolio."

William Berstein
The Intelligent Asset Allocator, p 50

Chapter 25
Fixed Income Investing

Abstract - Short-term bonds have less volatility and lower correlation to equities than long-term bonds. Bonds with maturities over 5 years don't offer sufficient reward for their higher risk.

Fixed income securities should be included in most, if not all, individual investors' portfolios.

Eugene Fama in *Time Varying Expected Returns* (Feb 1988, unpublished paper, data updated regularly) studies the returns of bonds. He finds that the time premium for longer term bonds is not reliable; that is, long term bonds have widely variable rates of return. He also finds that bonds with maturities beyond five years don't offer sufficient reward for their higher risk.

Dimensional Fund Advisors (DFA) has confirmed the poor return/risk characteristics of long term bonds from 1964-2005. DFA (in agreement with Fama) finds increases in yields from increasing maturity weakens beyond five years maturity.

TABLE 25.1   FIXED INCOME RETURNS AND STANDARD DEVIATION

	Return	Standard Deviation
1 month Treasury Bill	5.83%	1.35%
6 month Treasury Bill	6.59%	1.74%
1 year Treasury Bill	6.78%	2.37%
5 year Treasury Note	7.44%	6.27%
20 year Govt Bonds	7.61%	10.97%

Maturities for all fixed income funds (or portfolios) should therefore be kept to about five years.

If your fixed income allocation is less than $500,000, the best way to invest in bonds is through short-term bond index funds (or ETFs). But if you have more than $500,000 in fixed income, you might consider creating your own portfolio. You can do it yourself (you will need a lot of technical bond know how), use a "separate account manager" or use your financial advisor (if he has the ability).

A $500,000 bond portfolio will allow you to buy ten individual bonds; accomplishing both diversification and holding down trading costs (smaller purchases would have much higher trading costs and fewer than ten bonds would not be diversified enough). A "laddered" bond portfolio with ten individual $50,000 bonds each with maturities from one to ten years would have an average maturity of 5.5 years. Each year as one bond matures you replace it with a new ten year bond, re-extending the portfolio maturity to 5.5 years.

You will be able to achieve a little better return on your bond investments by constructing your own portfolio, but some of this advantage will be eroded by the cost of an investment advisor or separate account manager. The easiest way to invest in bonds for most of us is still through short-term bond index funds (or ETFs).

Investing in global bonds can increase diversification.

Chapter 26
Real Estate and Commodities
Asset Class Investing

Abstract - Real Estate Investment Trusts (REITs) and commodities tend to have low correlation with equities and fixed income and therefore provide useful diversification in a modern portfolio. REITs can in addition provide important dividend income in retirement. Overall they haven't added much return (or have even depressed returns a little) but together may add important diversification in difficult market periods. Many of you will choose to forego these asset classes. I do not hold them in my own portfolio, but felt they needed to be covered in the discussion.

Most asset allocation discussions focus mainly (or even only) on stocks, bonds and cash. Two alternative asset classes will be discussed in this chapter: real estate and commodities. Each can play a unique role. The easiest way to invest in real estate is in a Real Estate Investment Trust (REIT) mutual fund; commodities are a little less easily available.

A REIT pays no corporate income tax as long as it distributes at least 90% of its taxable income and generates at least 75% of that income from rents, mortgages and sales of property. This unique tax treatment causes REIT's to spin off a lot of income (a useful asset attribute after retirement). Before retirement, it may be best to hold them in tax deferred accounts.

Real Estate assets tend to perform well in periods of high inflation, when the replacement cost of real estate is driven up. Inflation, at the same time, tends to drive down the price of stocks and bonds. Bonds tend to do poorly in inflation, but they provide great protection and performance during periods of deflation. Real estate assets tend to have low correlations with equities in general.

Real estate returns and risks in general tend to fall between those of equities and fixed income. REIT's over the last 30 years have outperformed their long-term averages. Future returns are likely to be nearer long-term averages. Following the recent tech bubble collapse, significant amounts of cash flowed from the equities market into real estate; creating what many argue is now a real estate bubble. The very existence of this pattern is strong evidence of negative correlation.

Two REIT mutual funds stand out among the available publicly traded real estate securities: Vanguard's VGSIX (1996 inception) and DFA's DFREX (1992 inception). Their performance has been relatively similar.

Many expect future returns to be dampened by a correction in the real estate market (bubble or no, regression to the mean is likely to happen).

Commodities are not capital or financial assets. Like real estate, they are real assets; stuff you can touch. Commodities can be segmented into "hard" non-perishable commodities (like oil, gas, gold, silver, aluminum, copper and timber) and "soft" perishable or consumable commodities (like coffee, corn, wheat, soybeans and livestock).

There are three ways to gain exposure to commodities: a) direct purchase of the actual "stuff," b) a portfolio of commodity-related stocks and c) commodities (futures) index funds. The first two are problematic. Buying the actual stuff is an absurd idea for nearly all of us; and commodity-related stocks tend to behave more like stocks than the underlying commodities. That leaves commodities (futures) index funds. These index funds invest in fully collateralized commodity futures (meaning that for every dollar invested in futures, a dollar is also invested in something like 3 month treasury bills). The total return includes return on the collateral investment. Even though commodities futures have been traded in the US for over 100 years, they are surrounded by a lot of confusion.

With the guy on TV telling you that a fortune can be made in unleaded gas futures because the price of gas is about to go up and all the goofy stuff going on in the world of hedge funds, what's needed is some clarity; two recent academic studies have begun to provide just that. The first by Gary Gorton (The Wharton School) and K. Geert Rouwenhorst (Yale University), *Facts and Fantasies about Commodities Futures* published in 2005, began to address a number of important questions. They conclude:

> *"commodities futures returns have been especially effective in providing diversification of stock and bond portfolios. The correlation with stocks and bonds is negative over most horizons, and the negative correlation is stronger over longer holding periods."*

The second by Ibbotson Associates, *Strategic Asset Allocation and Commodities* published in 2006, studied the role of commodities in investment portfolio allocations. They found that from 1970 to 2004, commodities provided higher average and total returns than US and international stocks and US and international bonds with a standard deviation between US and international stocks. In addition they also find that commodities futures are negatively correlated with ALL of these asset classes (except international bonds). In addition to the generally negative correlation, commodities performed best when you needed them most; providing the highest return of any asset class in the study in the 8 years when equities had negative returns and the 2 years when bonds had negative returns.

The three most widely used commodities indexes are the Goldman Sachs Commodities Index (GSCI), the Dow Jones-AIG Commodity Index (DJ-AIG), and the Reuters/Jeffries CRB Index (RJ-CRB). In addition to these three commercially available indexes, the Ibbotson study analyzes the Gorton and Rouwenhorst Commodity Index (creating an Ibbotson Composite Commodity Index from a combination of all four (to reduce the impact of sector weightings in any one index). The available indexes vary widely in their sector weighting.

There is considerable disparity in the returns and risk characteristics of each of these indices. More indices are being added each year. Important among these are the Standard and Poors Commodity Index (S&P CI); The Rogers International Commodity Index (RICI) and the Deutsche Bank Commodity Index (DBCI).

Currently neither Vanguard nor DFA offers an index mutual fund tracking a commodities index. Commodities index mutual funds are very limited. The first funds on the scene were the Oppenheimer Real Asset Fund (QRAAX: 1997 inception actively managed front end loaded fund) and PIMCO's Commodity Real Return Strategy (PCRDX: inception 2002; the first passively managed no-load fund). PCRDX tracks the DJ-AIG commodities index. ETFs may be a better commodities mousetrap (discussed in the next chapter).

Commodities Index tracking ETFs include:

GSG	iShares	tracking the Goldman Sachs CI (GSCI)
DBC	Powershares	tracking the Deutsche Bank CI (DBCI)

The returns of these asset classes since 1992 are shown below:

TABLE 26.1   REITs and COMMODITIES RETURNS

		S&P 500	REIT's DFA DFREX	GSCI Com Index	Bond Returns Ibottson Intermed	Ibottson Long-Term
	1992	7.7	28.3	4.4	7.2	8.1
	1993	10.0	22.5	-12.3	11.2	18.2
	1994	1.3	3.6	5.3	-5.1	-7.8
	1995	37.4	12.1	20.3	16.1	31.7
	1996	23.1	33.8	33.9	2.1	-0.9
	1997	33.4	19.4	-14.1	8.4	15.9
	1998	28.6	-15.4	-35.8	10.2	13.1
	1999	21.0	-2.0	40.9	-1.8	-9.0
90's Bull Market	Average Return	20.3	12.8	5.3	6.0	8.7
	Annualized Return	19.7	11.7	2.4	5.8	7.9
	Growth of $1,000	$4,212	$2,418	$1,208	$1,574	$1,833
	2000	-9.1	28.4	49.7	12.6	21.5
	2001	-11.9	13.2	-31.9	5.4	3.7
	2002	-22.1	4.2	32.1	14.8	17.8
Bear Market	Average Return	-14.4	15.3	16.6	10.9	14.3
	Annualized Return	-14.6	14.8	10.4	10.8	14.1
	Growth of $1,000	$624	$1,515	$1,346	$1,362	$1,484
	2003	28.7	35.6	20.7	2.1	1.5
	2004	10.9	32.1	17.3	6.0	9.4
	2005	4.9	13.2	22.6	3.7	6.6
	2006	15.6	35.3	-15.1	3.2	2.7
Recovery	Average Return	15.0	29.0	11.4	3.8	5.0
	Annualized Return	14.7	28.7	10.2	3.8	5.0
	Growth of $1,000	$1,731	$2,743	$1,473	$1,159	$1,215
Bear + Recovery	Average Return	2.4	23.1	13.6	6.8	9.0
	Annualized Return	1.1	22.6	10.3	6.7	8.8
	Growth of $1,000	$1,080	$4,154	$1,983	$1,578	$1,803
1992 to 2006	Average Return	12.0	17.6	9.2	6.4	8.8
	Annualized Return	10.6	16.6	6.0	6.3	8.3
	Standard Deviation	17.4	15.3	26.2	6.0	11.1
	Growth of $1,000	$4,549	$10,043	$2,397	$2,484	$3,305
1975 to 2006 (32 years)	Average Return	14.6	18.4	10.2	8.5	9.9
	Annualized Return	13.5	17.4	7.9	8.3	9.3
	Standard Deviation	15.7	15.4	22.1	6.8	12.0
	Growth of $1,000	$57,644	$170,222	$11,337	$12,870	$16,973
	Expected Future Average Return	9.5				
	Expected Future Standard Deviation	16.0				
	Average Projected 30 yr Growth of $1,000	12,087				

If commodities futures give you the "willies" then don't bother with them. You can create a very good portfolio without them (or REITs); and sleeping well is important also.

Chapter 27
Exchange Traded Funds (ETFs)

Abstract - ETFs have exploded onto the market in the new millennium. While they have low expense ratios and some tax efficiency, the costs of trading (commissions and bid-ask spreads) can make them unattractive for many buy and hold investors making regular contributions to their nestegg. If your company plan doesn't include index funds, ETFs may be useful.

Exchange Traded Funds are portfolios of stocks or bonds that track a specific market index such as the S&P 500 or the MSCI EAFE; or a market sector such as energy or technology; or a commodity such as gold, silver or petroleum. Like stocks, ETFs can be bought and sold on a stock exchange throughout the trading day. You can buy or sell them in almost any brokerage account (in exactly the same ways you can buy and sell stocks, including online trading).

The advantages are: 1) low expense ratios, 2) tax efficiency and 3) liquidity.

The disadvantages are: 1) commissions for each trade and 2) ETFs have bid-ask spreads (you get nicked a little on each trade – see chapter 13). These trading costs are substantial.

Wilfred L. Dellva, of Villanova University, found that an online investor (lowest commissions) with a $10,000 ETF investment must hold the investment into the sixth year to overcome the trading costs (a retail brokerage investor must hold a similar investment nine years). With over a $100,000 ETF investment, the picture changes. Commissions can become nearly negligible.

ETFs are more tax efficient than most mutual funds because they are not forced to "cash out" investors by selling assets (an investor simply sells his ETF shares in the market). But they will have capital gains distributions from time to time. ETFs that are more likely to have capital gains distributions are those that track indexes that are less static. Small cap and value oriented indexes tend to have built-in outmigration as stocks grow larger or change book-to-market value.

For tax sensitive investors, a tax-managed mutual fund may make more sense. In a tax-deferred investment account, ETFs make even less sense. There is no tax efficiency at all to overcome the cost of commissions.

Major issuers of ETFs include Barclays Global Investors (iShares), State Street Global Advisors (streetTRACKS), Vanguard Group (VIPERS), Rydex Financial (Rydex ETFs), Powershares and Wisdomtree. The top ETFs by assets under management are SPDRS "Spiders" (SPY), iShares MSCI EAFE Index (EFA), NASDAQ 100 "qubes" (QQQQ), iShares S&P 500 (IVV), iShares MSCI Japan (EWJ), iShares Emerging Markets (EEM)

The explosive growth of ETFs has created a lot of goofy new market segments and "indexes". Some of these have significant management fees and make no sense for a modern portfolio asset class index fund investor. If you invest in ETFs, stick to the asset classes discussed in the following chapter and included in the model portfolios in the next section; then buy in one lump sum and hold them.

ETFs are available covering indexes for many useful basic asset classes (and far too many less than useful new proto-asset classes). Chapter 33 suggests a group of iShares ETFs for basic asset class holdings. ETFs will be especially important to you if your company plan doesn't include index funds.

Most of you should stick to index mutual funds.

Part Four

Modern Portfolio Management

Chapter 28

Asset Allocation

Abstract -   Asset allocation is the single most important determinant of investment returns. More than 90% of return variability is explained by asset allocation. Modern index funds allow diversification into the asset classes we reviewed earlier: fixed income, US lg cap, US sm cap, US lg value, US sm value and international equities (lg, small, lg value, sm value and emerging markets). Diversification into all of these asset classes will increase your return and decrease your risk at the same time. This is the "free lunch" of modern portfolio theory.

Three important academic studies have looked at the impact of asset allocation on portfolio performance. The landmark study, *Determinants of Portfolio Performance*, Financial Analysts Journal, July-August 1991, by Brinson, Hood and Beebower and a follow up study in 1996 by Brinson, Hood and Singer essentially confirmed that 93.6% of the portfolio's return and risk were determined by its asset allocation (stock selection and market timing were only minor influences in comparison). These studies caused quite a stir among the stock pickers and market timers of the world (no small group) as can be seen from the title of a recent study on the subject: *Does Asset Allocation Explain 40, 90 or 100 Percent of Performance*, by Paul Kaplan, Financial Analysts Journal, January-February 2001. The study overwhelmingly confirmed that more than 90% of a portfolio's long term variation in return was explained by its asset allocation.

The risk/return plots included below show the impact on returns and standard deviation (risk) resulting from combining two asset classes together. Returns are on the vertical axis and standard deviation (risk) on the horizontal axis. The goal is to move your portfolio up and to the left, that is, increase return and reduce risk. The limit of movement in that direction is called the "efficient frontier" (the Holy Grail of modern portfolio theory investing).

Remember, at this point we are looking for a large number of asset classes. Climbing any individual curve to its limit is self defeating (it would result in a concentrated, very risky, portfolio). Each point on the curve represents an additional 10% of the added asset class. Since we are looking at around 10 equities related asset classes we can only climb any one curve by one or two points (10% to 20%).

The first, and in some ways most important, asset allocation decision you should tackle is how much fixed income you will hold in your portfolio. This is basically a risk question. More fixed income equals less risk; less fixed income equals more risk.

A.   How much fixed income?

The spectrum normally runs from 10% to 50% of the total portfolio. Very few will reasonably fall outside this range. As a rule of thumb: 10% for accumulators; 25% for very early retirees (still in their 50's) and consequently with very long time horizons; 40% for most retirees in their 60's; and 50% for retirees in their 70's and older with short time horizons is a good place to start. Two other common ways to look at it are: a) your age less 25 as a goal for your fixed income allocation; or b) 120 less your age as a good equities allocation goal. They all yield similar, but not identical results.

While the returns of fixed income are low, they act as a shock absorber in a modern portfolio. As you can see in the figure below, your risk is reduced (movement to the left) more than your return is reduced as you add fixed income to your portfolio.

FIGURE 28.1   FIXED INCOME/S&P 500   RISK/RETURN PLOT (1975 to 2006)

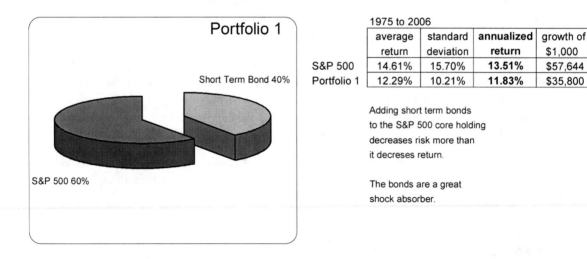

To analyze the beneficial impact of various asset classes, we are going to start with a very simple portfolio, combining 60% S&P 500 and 40% short term bonds. If you aren't comfortable with much risk, the 40% fixed income allocation is a good place to start. If you are more comfortable with taking on some risk, you may want to allocate less than 40% (say 25% or even 10%) to fixed income. Returns (and risk) for portfolios based on 10%, 25%, 40% and 50% fixed income allocations are outlined in the following chapters. In this chapter we will look only at the 40% fixed income allocation. A good basic benchmark portfolio.

Portfolio 1

Short Term Bond 40%

S&P 500 60%

1975 to 2006

	average return	standard deviation	annualized return	growth of $1,000
S&P 500	14.61%	15.70%	**13.51%**	$57,644
Portfolio 1	12.29%	10.21%	**11.83%**	$35,800

Adding short term bonds to the S&P 500 core holding decreases risk more than it decreses return.

The bonds are a great shock absorber.

You can see that you have given up some return; but the ride will be a lot smoother. This is not a bad portfolio. Simple portfolios like this should be taken seriously. They are boring; but they will keep you out of trouble. You will see later that this portfolio would have done pretty well (especially through the recent bear market from 2000 to 2002).

But you can do better without more risk. Watch what happens to this portfolio as we add asset classes. More returns, less risk, better growth of $1,000 invested.

B.   How much international?

A 30% to 40% international allocation (of total equities) is a good place to start. For the example we are developing here we are going to use 40%. I have used 50% in my own personal nestegg. International equities have been a good investment over the last 30 years (very good over the last 10 years) and are likely to continue to perform well into the future. Because the rest of the world is likely to have a higher rate of growth than the U.S., a large allocation of your equities to international may be very important in the long term. In addition, a large international allocation guards against the negative impact of the probable continuing depreciation of the dollar.

FIGURE 28.2   INT'L LARGE CAP/S&P 500   RISK/RETURN PLOT (1975 to 2006)

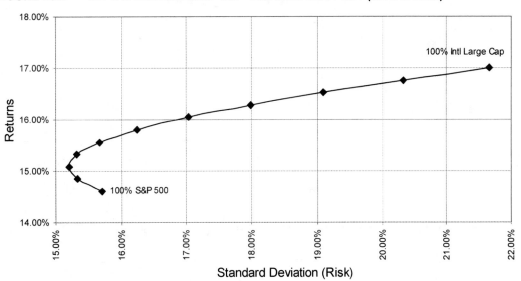

Portfolio 2 adds International large cap (dividing equities into 60% US and 40% International). The benefit is all positive. Increased return with decreased risk. This is the "free lunch" of modern portfolio theory.

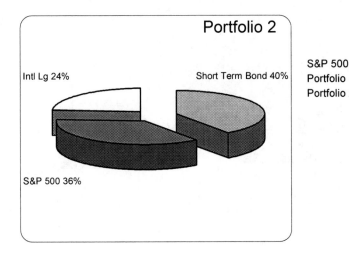

	1975 to 2006			
	average return	standard deviation	**annualized return**	growth of $1,000
S&P 500	14.61%	15.70%	**13.51%**	$57,644
Portfolio 1	12.29%	10.21%	**11.83%**	$35,800
Portfolio 2	12.86%	9.97%	**12.43%**	$42,457

Adding International equities
increases return and
decreases risk

Next we will take advantage of the persistent size and value premium.

D.   How much small cap?

The spectrum normally runs from 10% to 50% (or more) of US and International equities. I am inclined to use a 50% small cap allocation across the board (50% of US and 50% of International.

FIGURE 28.3   US SMALL CAP/S&P 500   RISK/RETURN PLOT (1975 to 2006)

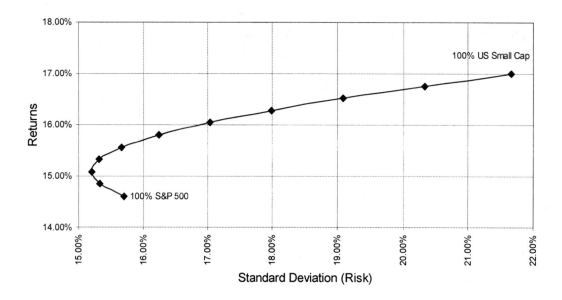

FIGURE 28.4   INTL SMALL CAP/S&P 500   RISK/RETURN PLOT (1975 to 2006)

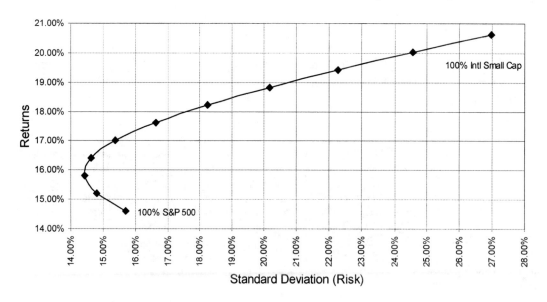

Adding US and International small cap provides a very dramatic benefit; strongly increased return, with a negligible increase in risk.

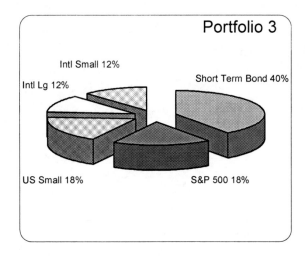

1975 to 2006	average return	standard deviation	annualized return	growth of $1,000
S&P 500	14.61%	15.70%	**13.51%**	$57,644
Portfolio 1	12.29%	10.21%	**11.83%**	$35,800
Portfolio 2	12.86%	9.97%	**12.43%**	$42,457
Portfolio 3	14.04%	9.90%	**13.62%**	$59,471

Adding small cap equities strongly increases return with a small decrease in risk

Even though the average return of this portfolio is still less than the S&P 500, the dramatic decrease in volatility results in a higher annualized return and therefore in the growth of $1,000 invested. This was Harry Markowitz' Nobel Prize winning insight. This is the "free lunch" of modern portfolio theory investing.

E.   How much value?

The spectrum normally runs from 10% to 50% (or more) of US equities. Over the past 30 years, the value premium has been quite strong, and the risk has been quite low. Because of its very strong performance, many advise a strong "value tilt" including an over representation of this asset class. A 50% allocation of all your US and International equities to value is a good place to start, adding to long term return and reducing risk.

FIGURE 28.5   US LARGE VALUE/S&P 500   RISK/RETURN PLOT (1975 to 2006)

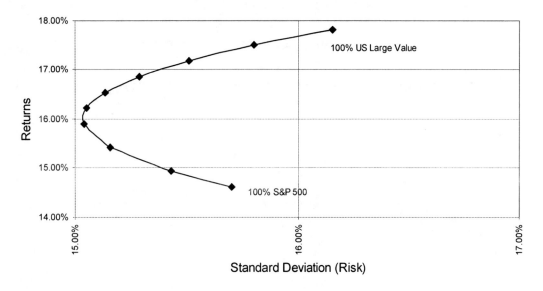

The value premium extends across size and international equities.

FIGURE 28.6   US SMALL CAP VALUE/S&P 500   RISK/RETURN PLOT (1975 to 2006)

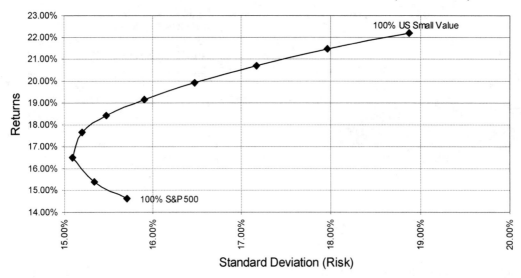

FIGURE 28.7   INTL LARGE VALUE/S&P 500   RISK/RETURN PLOT (1975 to 2006)

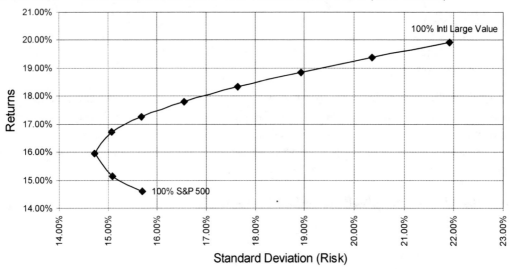

FIGURE 28.8   EMERGING MARKETS/S&P 500   RISK/RETURN PLOT (1995 to 2006)

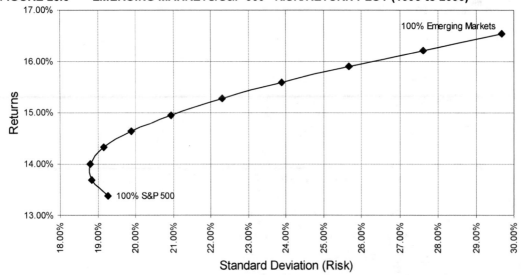

Portfolio 4 adds 50% value in both large and small cap, in both US and International plus a 20% allocation of international equities to emerging markets.

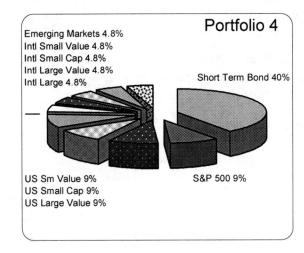

1975 to 2006

	average return	standard deviation	annualized return	growth of $1,000
S&P 500	14.61%	15.70%	**13.51%**	$57,644
Portfolio 1	12.29%	10.21%	**11.83%**	$35,800
Portfolio 2	12.86%	9.97%	**12.43%**	$42,457
Portfolio 3	14.04%	9.90%	**13.62%**	$59,471
Portfolio 4	14.78%	9.87%	**14.37%**	$73,420

Adding value & Emerging Markets strongly increases return with no change in risk

Note: Portfolio 4 finally has an **average** return 0.17% higher than the S&P 500. The **annualized** return exceeded the S&P 500 with Portfolio 3. Annualized return 0.86% higher than the S&P 500 drives the real growth of your money to $73,420 (27.37% higher than the S&P 500)

C. How much US Real Estate and Commodities?

Not everyone will be comfortable adding real estate and commodities to their portfolio.

The spectrum for REITs runs from 0% to 20% of your US equities. I am inclined to add some Real Estate because of its diversification value and dividend income. REITs have demonstrated extremely low correlation with equities in the last ten years. Adding some to your portfolio will likely add return and reduce risk.

The research on commodities index investing is quite compelling. The Goldman Sachs Commodities Index (GSCI) has demonstrated equities like returns that have been negatively (not just poorly) correlated with the stocks and bonds.

The spectrum for commodities indexes runs from 0% to 25% of the whole portfolio. The research on these assets while compelling is still somewhat new; and I have not yet added commodities to my own portfolio.

Visit *www.retireearlysleepwell.com* for more information on REITs and commodities investing issues.

Summary

You can see from the growth of $1,000 investment in each of these portfolios how much improvement in results comes from apparently very small improvements in return and risk. Football is often said to be a game of inches. Well so is investment. Work hard to diversify and the small improvement in return and risk will translate into solid nestegg growth and protection.

You can avoid the risk of a concentrated portfolio and still increase your returns by combining a variety of asset classes in a portfolio. Past performance is not a guaranty of future performance; in fact returns in the future are likely to be a lot lower, as we have reviewed earlier. But the relative performance of portfolio diversification is likely to be very persistent.

Portfolios 1 through 4 all use asset class return and risk data based on CRSP and Dimensional Fund Advisors (DFA) research and information. So far only DFA has developed index mutual funds that track these tightly defined sophisticated asset classes. Vanguard has developed a lot of good index funds, many that appear similar to the DFA funds; but with no micro cap stocks, less deep value and no small cap value international at all.

You can see in the following scatter chart (Figure 28.9) how these portfolios relate to the risk and returns of the underlying asset classes over the last 30 years. This is a graphic depiction of the insight that won the Nobel Prize for Harry Markowitz.

FIGURE 28.9   RISK RETURN SCATTER PLOT (1975 to 2006)

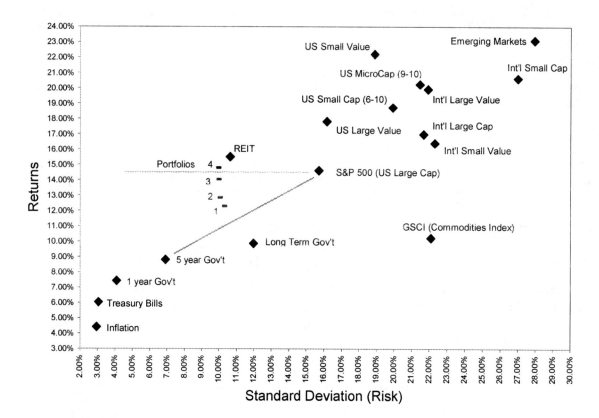

There are endless model portfolios, endless potential mean variance optimization analyses, and endless personality and risk tolerance profiling options available to you. The actual choice of a specific portfolio is far less important than your ability to buy it and then hold it; even when the market gets weird. Mean variance optimization analyzes alternative combinations of asset allocations (classes and percentage allocations) to determine the "best" allocation for a given set of returns, correlations and standard deviation data. In the end even a simple naïve portfolio will do quite well.

Three alternative approaches follow in the next chapters. The first two are available to everyone through Vanguard. The last two are available only through investment advisors approved by DFA Funds. The DFA funds do better at reaching into the value and small cap premiums.

In 1975 only an S&P 500 index would have been available. Vanguard and DFA now offer a very good selection of asset class index funds. Since many were not created until the 90's, the portfolios in the next three chapters use estimated historical returns based on the performance of the underlying asset class benchmarks (for which good data is available back to 1975). See Appendix D for details.

Chapter 29
The Simplified Modern Portfolio
using Vanguard index mutual funds

Abstract - If you want to keep it simple, four Vanguard index funds can provide basic diversification – a simplified basic modern portfolio.

In 1991, Scott Burns, a syndicated financial columnist with the Dallas Morning News, introduced his "Couch Potato Portfolio" (containing only two funds). 50% Vanguard 500 index (VFINX) and 50% Vanguard Total Bond Market Index (VBMFX). Simple enough?

Paul B. Farrell's, *The Lazy Person's Guide to Investing*, is a guide to a variety of these Lazy-boy approaches to modern portfolio theory. In it he recounts a conversation between Scott Burns and Harry Markowitz. Burns asked Markowitz how he invested his own personal retirement funds. Markowitz' answer: "I should have computed co-variances of the asset classes and drawn an efficient frontier; instead, I split my contributions 50/50 between bonds and equities [to] minimize my future regret". Priceless. Harry Markowitz may be a couch potato investor.

The **"Simplified Modern Portfolio"** is only a little more complicated, adding some exposure to US Small Value and International Equities. This 4 fund alternative is a very powerful alternative that will work for most people; providing a little more return and a little more diversification (lower risk) than the couch potato portfolio.

TABLE 29.1   THE SIMPLIFIED MODERN PORTFOLIO

						Allocations
Money Mkt	VMMXX	Money Mkt six months of average expenses				
Fixed Income	(percent of **total portfolio**)		10%	25%	40%	50%
	VBISX	Short Term Bond Index		100%	of fixed income	
Equities	(percent of **total portfolio**)		90%	75%	60%	50%
U.S. Equities	(percent of **equities**)			60%	of equities	
	VFINX	S&P 500 Index		50%	of US Equities	
	VISVX	Small Cap Value		50%	of US Equities	
Int'l Equities	(percent of **equities**)			40%	of equities	
	VGTSX	Total International Index		100%	of Int'l Equities	

These funds have a minimum investment of at least $1,000 each. If you have only two thousand to start with, divide it between VBISX and VFINX (go ahead, be a couch potato for a little while). Next year add international. Once you have all four asset classes covered you can begin to spread your investment to create the detailed allocation percentages you have established. At that point, all that's left is to rebalance once a year.

This very simple portfolio, with only four funds, performed well across a variety of periods.

TABLE 29.2   SIMPLIFIED MODERN PORTFOLIO RETURNS DATA

		S&P 500	Portfolio Fixed Income Percentages			
			10%	25%	40%	50%
	1992	7.7	7.9	7.7	7.6	7.4
	1993	10.0	23.3	20.8	18.3	16.6
	1994	1.3	4.1	3.3	2.6	2.1
	1995	37.4	23.0	21.3	19.6	18.5
	1996	23.1	14.6	12.9	11.2	10.1
	1997	33.4	19.5	17.4	15.3	14.0
	1998	28.6	11.8	11.1	10.4	9.9
	1999	21.0	17.6	15.0	12.4	10.7
90's Bull Market	Average Return	20.3	15.2	13.7	12.2	11.2
	Annualized Return	19.7	15.0	13.5	12.1	11.1
	Growth of $1,000	$4,212	$3,065	$2,763	$2,486	$2,315
	2000	-9.1	-1.3	0.4	2.1	3.3
	2001	-11.9	-5.9	-3.5	-1.0	0.6
	2002	-22.1	-14.6	-11.2	-7.7	-5.4
Bear Market	Average Return	-14.4	-7.3	-4.7	-2.2	-0.5
	Annualized Return	-14.6	-7.4	-4.9	-2.3	-0.6
	Growth of $1,000	$624	$793	$861	$933	$983
	2003	28.7	32.6	27.8	22.9	19.6
	2004	10.9	17.0	14.4	11.9	10.2
	2005	4.9	8.7	7.5	6.2	5.4
	2006	15.6	19.4	16.9	14.3	12.6
Recovery	Average Return	15.0	19.4	16.6	13.8	12.0
	Annualized Return	14.7	19.1	16.4	13.7	11.8
	Growth of $1,000	$1,731	$2,014	$1,836	$1,670	$1,565
Bear + Recovery	Average Return	2.4	8.0	7.5	7.0	6.6
	Annualized Return	1.1	6.9	6.8	6.5	6.3
	Growth of $1,000	$1,080	$1,597	$1,581	$1,557	$1,538
1992 to 2006	Average Return	12.0	11.8	10.8	9.7	9.0
	Annualized Return	10.6	11.2	10.3	9.4	8.8
	Standard Deviation	17.4	12.4	10.3	8.3	7.0
	Growth of $1,000	$4,549	$4,893	$4,367	$3,872	$3,559
1975 to 2006 (32 years)	Average Return	14.6	16.0	14.7	13.3	12.5
	Annualized Return	13.5	15.2	14.1	13.0	12.2
	Standard Deviation	15.7	13.5	11.4	9.5	8.3
	Growth of $1,000	$57,644	$92,397	$68,005	$49,264	$39,383
	Expected Future Average Return	10.0	10.0	9.1	8.2	7.6
	Expected Future Standard Deviation	17.0	13.1	11.1	9.2	8.1
	Average Projected 30 yr Growth of $1,000	13,401	14,970	12,530	10,195	8,813

This very simple portfolio would have served most investors very well through the last thirty years. How did your personal portfolio do across this period? Look in particular at the "Bear Market" and "Recovery" (2000-2006) period(s); note the growth of $1,000 over the period. There was no need to lose a lot of money. If you adopt a modern portfolio strategy (even this very simple one) you will have avoided the biggest problem encountered by most investors – losing money.

> *"Even though most investors see their work as active, assertive and on the offensive, the reality is, and should be, that stock and bond investing alike are primarily a defensive process. The great secret for success in long term investing is to avoid serious losses."*
>
> Charles Ellis, The Loser's Game, p 56

Chapter 30
The Do-it-yourself Modern Portfolio
The most powerful Vanguard portfolio

Abstract - If you want to do-it-yourself, Vanguard offers a family of funds that will allow you to take advantage of increased diversification into small cap, value and international equities and short-term bonds.

The growth of retail index funds in the last few years has greatly expanded the available alternatives. It is now possible to construct a good passive asset class index fund portfolio entirely from Vanguard (or several other families of funds – see Chapter 33).

TABLE 30.1   THE DO-IT-YOURSELF MODERN PORTFOLIO

Money Mkt	VMMXX	Money Mkt six months of average expenses				
						Allocations
Fixed Income	(percent of **total portfolio**)		10%	25%	40%	50%
	VBISX	Short-Term Bond Index		100%	of fixed income	
Equities	(percent of **total portfolio**)		90%	75%	60%	50%
U.S. Equities	(percent of **equities**)			**60%**	of equities	
	VFINX	S&P 500 Index			25%	of US Equities
	VIVAX	Value Index			25%	of US Equities
	NAESX	Small Cap			25%	of US Equities
	VISVX	Small Cap Value			25%	of US Equities
Int'l Equities	(percent of **equities**)			**40%**	of equities	
	VGTSX	Total International Index			50%	of Int'l Equities
	VTRIX	International Value			25%	of Int'l Equities
	VEIEX	Emerging Markets			25%	of Int'l Equities

This portfolio takes more advantage of the small cap and value premiums. The effect is significant. Remember a small increase in return can make a big difference alone; but decreasing volatility at the same time, will really give your investment nestegg a kick (over time).

In comparing the Simplified Modern Portfolios (in the previous chapter) to these more diversified Vanguard portfolios, look first at three things: 1) average return over the whole 1992 to 2005 period (increased for each fixed income allocation), 2) standard deviation over the whole period (decreased for each fixed income allocation) and 3) the growth of $1,000 invested over the whole period (a nice increase for each fixed income allocation).

The differences may look small, but over 30 years, it will add up to a very significant difference in lifestyle. You can see in figure 32.2 how comparative portfolios seem to hang together for a few years and then separate (by a lot) after the whole 30 years period. This figure's highest performers were from the next chapter's (DFA) modern power portfolios.

Working a little harder at diversification into small and value can have a big payoff.

These portfolios did even better across the variety of recent periods.

TABLE 30.2   DO-IT-YOURSELF MODERN PORTFOLIO RETURNS

		S&P 500	Portfolio Fixed Income Percentages			
			10%	25%	40%	50%
	1992	7.7	10.2	9.6	9.1	8.8
	1993	10.0	26.5	23.5	20.4	19.1
	1994	1.3	1.7	1.3	1.0	0.7
	1995	37.4	22.1	20.0	18.6	17.6
	1996	23.1	14.8	13.5	11.7	10.6
	1997	33.4	18.9	14.2	12.8	11.7
	1998	28.6	8.8	7.9	7.9	7.7
	1999	21.0	22.1	18.0	14.8	13.3
90's Bull Market	Average Return	20.3	15.6	13.5	12.0	11.2
	Annualized Return	19.7	15.4	13.3	11.9	11.1
	Growth of $1,000	$4,212	$3,139	$2,718	$2,455	$2,314
	2000	-9.1	-3.0	-0.9	1.1	2.1
	2001	-11.9	-5.6	-2.9	-0.6	1.0
	2002	-22.1	-14.6	-11.0	-7.6	-5.4
Bear Market	Average Return	-14.4	-7.7	-4.9	-2.4	-0.8
	Annualized Return	-14.6	-7.9	-5.0	-2.4	-0.8
	Growth of $1,000	$624	$782	$856	$929	$976
	2003	28.7	36.2	30.5	25.1	22.1
	2004	10.9	17.8	14.8	12.2	10.7
	2005	4.9	10.7	9.3	7.7	6.9
	2006	15.6	20.1	17.4	14.7	13.3
Recovery	Average Return	15.0	21.2	18.0	14.9	13.2
	Annualized Return	14.7	20.8	17.8	14.8	13.1
	Growth of $1,000	$1,731	$2,132	$1,923	$1,734	$1,637
Bear + Recovery	Average Return	2.4	8.8	8.2	7.5	7.2
	Annualized Return	1.1	7.6	7.4	7.0	6.9
	Growth of $1,000	$1,080	$1,667	$1,647	$1,611	$1,597
1992 to 2006	Average Return	12.0	12.4	11.0	9.9	9.3
	Annualized Return	10.6	11.7	10.5	9.6	9.1
	Standard Deviation	17.4	13.4	10.9	8.7	7.5
	Growth of $1,000	$4,549	$5,232	$4,476	$3,954	$3,695
1975 to 2006 (32 years)	Average Return	14.6	16.5	15.4	13.9	13.2
	Annualized Return	13.5	15.7	14.7	13.5	12.9
	Standard Deviation	15.7	14.0	11.8	9.8	8.7
	Growth of $1,000	$57,644	$106,073	$81,538	$57,186	$47,943
Expected Future Average Return		10.0	10.8	9.8	8.8	8.1
Expected Future Standard Deviation		17.0	13.0	11.0	9.2	8.1
Average Projected 30 yr Growth of $1,000		13,401	18,805	15,123	11,917	10,095

Note the improvement in performance over the Simplified Portfolios. Note also the failure to reach the performance of the benchmark Portfolio 4. The reason is the lack of exposure to critical asset classes in the available Vanguard index funds. The lack is in three main areas: 1) international small cap and small cap value, 2) lack of exposure to micro cap (deciles 9-10) in the Vanguard small cap indexes and 3) lack of exposure to deep value (see Chapter 23 page 54).

Still, this is a very good portfolio.

You can contact Vanguard directly at *www.vanguard.com* or 800-831-9996 to obtain information about their funds. You should be careful to look for new funds that fill in their weaknesses in the future.

Chapter 31
The Modern DFA Power Portfolio
using Dimensional Fund Advisors (DFA) index mutual funds

Abstract - The Modern Power Portfolio provides a portfolio of DFA funds. DFA has designed a whole family of specialized index funds based on the Nobel Prize winning strategies of modern portfolio theory. To gain access to these funds, individuals must retain the services of an independent financial advisor approved by DFA.

Dimensional Fund Advisors (DFA) was founded in 1981 offering modern portfolio theory index funds to institutional investors. DFA now offers over 30 low cost asset class index funds based on the research we have just reviewed. These funds are available to individuals only through financial advisors. A limited group of financial advisors has been approved by DFA. Each must demonstrate a commitment to buy-and-hold passive asset class index fund investing. Their fees are an additional cost to individual DFA investors. Whether it makes sense to pay these fees to gain access to DFA is the subject of some debate. Fees range from flat fees of a few thousand dollars per year to percentage fees of 0.5% to 1.25% of assets under management. DFA funds have a minimum investment of $3,000.

TABLE 31.1   THE MODERN POWER PORTFOLIO

Money Mkt	VMMXX	Money Mkt six months of average expenses				
						Allocations
Fixed Income		(percent of **total portfolio**)	10%	25%	40%	50%
	DFIHX	One Year Fixed Income		10%	of fixed income	
	DFFGX	Five Year Gov't Fixed Income		40%	of fixed income	
	DFGFX	Two Year Global Fixed Income		10%	of fixed income	
	DFGBX	Five Year Global Fixed Income		40%	of fixed income	
Equities		(percent of **total portfolio**)	90%	75%	60%	50%
U.S. Equities		(percent of **equities**)		**60%**	of equities	
	DFLCX	US Lg Cap (S&P 500 Index)		25%	of US Equities	
	DFLVX	US Lg Value Index		25%	of US Equities	
	DFSTX	US Small Cap (6-10 decile)		12.5%	of US Equities	
	DFSCX	US Micro Cap (9-10 decile)		12.5%	of US Equities	
	DFSVX	US Small Cap Value Index		25%	of US Equities	
Int'l Equities		(percent of **equities**)		**40%**	of equities	
	DFALX	Int'l Lg Cap Index		20%	of Int'l Equities	
	DFIVX	Int'l Lg Cap Value Index		20%	of Int'l Equities	
	DFISX	Int'l Small Cap Index		20%	of Int'l Equities	
	DISVX	Int'l Small Cap Value Index		20%	of Int'l Equities	
	DFEMX	Emerging Markets Index		20%	of Int'l Equities	

The Modern Power Portfolio above uses DFA funds to reach into very small cap and into deep value (both in the US and international markets). This is not yet possible with Vanguard's funds.

TABLE 31.2   DFA MODERN POWER PORTFOLIO RETURNS

		S&P 500	Portfolio Fixed Income Percentages			
			10%	25%	40%	50%
	1992	7.7	9.9	9.4	8.8	8.4
	1993	10.0	26.2	23.3	20.4	18.5
	1994	1.3	1.5	0.8	0.2	-0.3
	1995	37.4	21.8	20.1	18.5	17.4
	1996	23.1	14.1	13.1	12.1	11.5
	1997	33.4	14.5	13.3	12.0	11.2
	1998	28.6	7.0	7.0	6.9	6.9
	1999	21.0	20.7	17.9	15.1	13.2
90's Bull Market	Average Return	20.3	14.5	13.1	11.8	10.8
	Annualized Return	19.7	14.2	12.9	11.6	10.7
	Growth of $1,000	$4,212	$2,896	$2,640	$2,404	$2,256
	2000	-9.1	-1.8	-0.4	1.1	2.0
	2001	-11.9	0.9	1.8	2.7	3.3
	2002	-22.1	-9.3	-6.1	-2.9	-0.8
Bear Market	Average Return	-14.4	-3.4	-1.6	0.3	1.5
	Annualized Return	-14.6	-3.5	-1.6	0.3	1.5
	Growth of $1,000	$624	$899	$952	$1,008	$1,045
	2003	28.7	43.8	37.0	30.1	25.5
	2004	10.9	20.4	17.4	14.4	12.4
	2005	4.9	11.5	9.8	8.1	7.0
	2006	15.6	20.6	17.9	15.1	13.3
Recovery	Average Return	15.0	24.1	20.5	16.9	14.6
	Annualized Return	14.7	23.5	20.1	16.7	14.4
	Growth of $1,000	$1,731	$2,327	$2,081	$1,853	$1,711
Bear + Recovery	Average Return	2.4	12.3	11.0	9.8	9.0
	Annualized Return	1.1	11.1	10.3	9.3	8.7
	Growth of $1,000	$1,080	$2,092	$1,982	$1,867	$1,788
1992 to 2006	Average Return	12.0	13.5	12.2	10.8	10.0
	Annualized Return	10.6	12.8	11.7	10.5	9.7
	Standard Deviation	17.4	13.1	10.9	8.7	7.3
	Growth of $1,000	$4,549	$6,059	$5,233	$4,488	$4,035
1975 to 2006 (32 years)	Average Return	14.6	17.8	16.3	14.7	13.6
	Annualized Return	13.5	17.0	15.7	14.3	13.3
	Standard Deviation	15.7	14.0	11.8	9.8	8.5
	Growth of $1,000	$57,644	$152,336	$105,428	$71,701	$54,898
	Expected Future Average Return	10.0	11.6	10.4	9.3	8.5
	Expected Future Standard Deviation	17.0	12.8	10.9	9.0	7.9
	Average Projected 30 yr Growth of $1,000	13,401	23,526	18,180	13,784	11,448

These DFA portfolios dramatically outperformed the S&P500 over the last 30 years. Even the 50/50 and 60/40 asset allocations had 30 year growth of $1,000 exceeding the S&P 500. The 75/25 portfolio has twice the 30 year result of the S&P 500. The 90/10 portfolio has three times the S&P 500 30 year result. These are significant benefits!

The DFA funds faithfully track to CRSP decile based asset classes. The reason for the small difference from the benchmark Portfolio 4 relates to the introduction of shorter term fixed income (which marginally lowers return a little) and the US micro cap fund (which marginally increases return a little).

You can contact DFA directly at *www.dfafunds.com* to find approved advisors in your area. I have chosen to pay one of these advisors for his services to gain access to these extraordinary index funds. In addition to gaining access to these funds, you can establish a relationship with someone that can help you sort out all the noise in the markets and in the media.

Chapter 32
Model Portfolio Performance Summary

Abstract - The "irrational exuberance" of the late 90's created a bubble that caused a lot of heartache for anyone overexposed to the overperforming assets. Any of the model portfolios would have been easier to stay the course with than all S&P 500 (all NASDAQ was even more bizarre). In the end, the tortoise and the hare wound up together; but look closely at the race since 1999. The tortoise is the clear winner.

In the graph below, one Simplified portfolio, one Do-it-yourself portfolio, and three Modern Power portfolios are shown along with the S&P 500 for comparison.

Notice especially that the three year bear market was a **non-event** for the modern portfolios.

**FIGURE 32.1   MODEL PORTFOLIO PERFORMANCE   GROWTH OF $1,000
1992 to 2006**

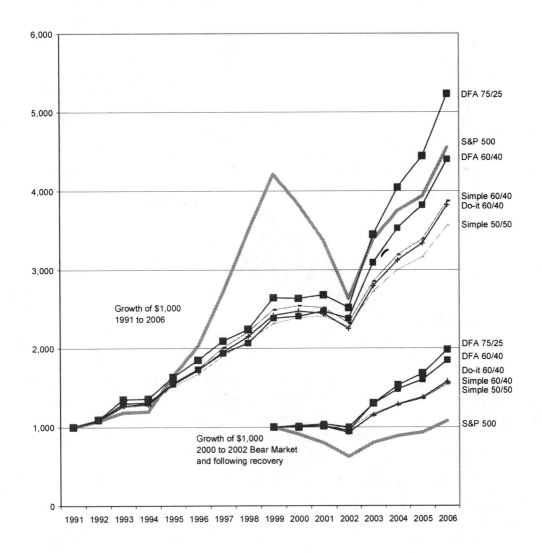

Thirty year performance for the Model Portfolios is shown in the graph below. The pre-inception performance of index funds is based on their benchmark indices for the period.

FIGURE 32.2 ESTIMATED 32 YEAR MODEL PORTFOLIO PERFORMANCE GROWTH OF $1,000   (1975 to 2006)

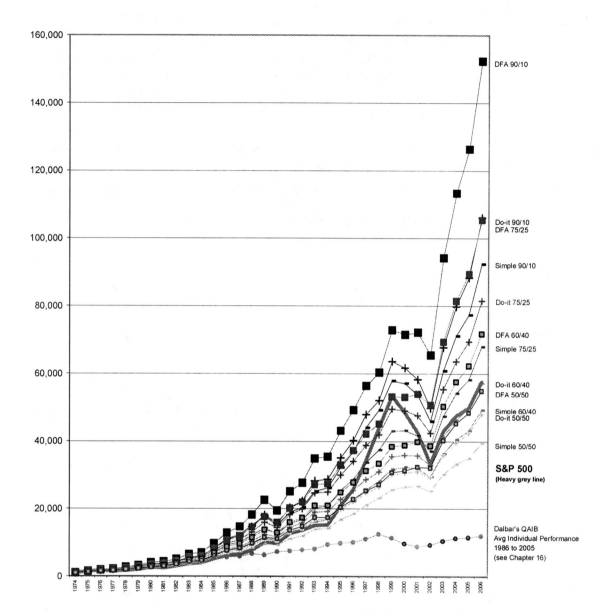

The average investor today is truly bewildered. Having missed most of the run from 1995-1999, he bought late (chasing performance); then rode it most of the way down. After a couple of years he sold (feeling he had to sell before he lost everything) and then stayed out of the market entirely for the next few years (missing the robust recovery). Today he looks at real estate and wishes he had bought 3 years ago. In the end, he has nothing to buy.

The right decision – buy everything and sleep well. How? You just read about it.

Even a 50% fixed income DFA portfolio was able to track the S&P 500. It would have been ahead until 1995 and the remarkable 5 year S&P 500 run at the end of 90's. But at the end of the full 30 year period they were together again. Most of us would not have been able to hold it through that run; and would been more comfortable if we held a 60/40 or 75/25 portfolio.

The following scatter chart shows the risk/return relationship of the model portfolios and underlying asset classes.

**FIGURE 32.3   ASSET CLASS RISK RETURN SCATTER PLOT (1975 to 2006)
with Vanguard and DFA PORTFOLIO PERFORMANCE**

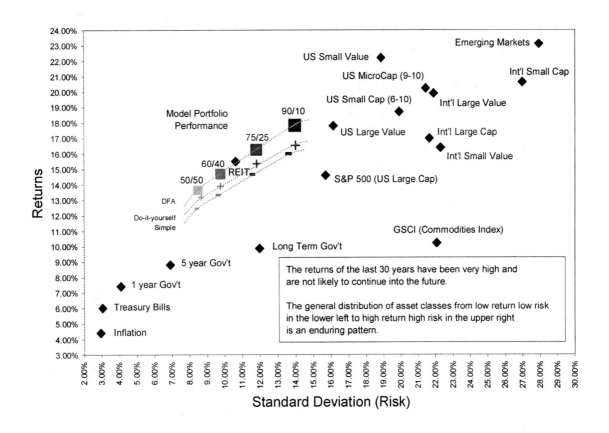

Chapter 33
Making the Most of Your Plan's Funds

Abstract - The strategy outlined below will allow you to apply the principles of modern portfolio theory to the limited number of funds available in your company retirement plan.

If your company's retirement plan limits you to a small group of funds you must select from, you can still put together a modern portfolio. The steps below will help you sort through the funds available to you.

Your first task is always to select the asset classes you want to hold in your portfolio (Chapter 28). You should always look for index funds, or funds with the lowest expenses.

Step One: Find a short term bond fund. You are looking for average and maturity of from two to five years, but seven years is okay. Choose an index fund if it is available.

Step Two: Find a large cap fund (preferably an S&P 500 or Total Market index fund).

You will be able to complete steps one and two in almost every family of funds. If you can go no further, don't be too disappointed. A simple mix of short term bonds and large cap stocks is still a very good portfolio.

If you can go on to step three below you will improve your diversification (improving returns and reducing risk).

Step Three: Try to find a real estate, large value, small cap, small-cap value and international asset class funds.

Most of you will find at least one or more of these asset classes. Some will find two, or three, or more. Depending on how many "step three" funds you have available, you can choose one of the portfolios from the preceding Chapters as a pattern for your portfolio allocation.

Mongrel Portfolios (close to the model portfolios) for several fund families are shown below. Most plans include access to a brokerage account where you can purchase ETFs.

TABLE 33.1   ETF BASED MODEL PORTFOLIO

Short Term Bond	SHY	iShares	Lehman 1-3 yr
Intermediate Term Bond	AGG	iShares	Lehman Aggregate Bond
Commodities	GSG	iShares	Goldman Sachs Commodities Index
Real Estate	ICF	iShares	Cohen and Steers Realty Majors
US Large Cap	IVV	iShares	S&P 500 Index
US Large Cap Value	IVE	iShares	S&P 500 Value Index
US Small Cap	IWM	iShares	Russell 2000 Index
US Small Cap Value	IWN	iShares	Russell 2000 Value Index
Intl Large Cap	EFA	iShares	MSCI EAFE Index
Intl Large Cap Value	EFV	iShares	MSCI EAFE Value Index
Intl Small Cap	DLS	Wisdomtree	International Small Dividend Fund
Intl Small Cap Value			*not available*
Emerging Markets	EEM	iShares	MSCI Emerging Markets

TABLE 33.2   SCHWAB PORTFOLIO

Short Term Bond	SWBDX	Schwab Short Term Bond Market
Intermediate Term Bond	SWLBX	Schwab Total Bond Market
Commodities	PCRDX	PIMCO Commodity Real Return Strategy D
Real Estate	CSRXX	Cohen & Steers Realty Shares
US Large Cap	SWPIX	Schwab S&P 500
US Large Cap Value	HRSVX	Heartland Select Value
US Small Cap	SWSMX	Schwab Small Cap Index
US Small Cap Value	HRTVX	Heartland Value
Intl Large Cap	SWINX	Schwab International Index
Intl Large Cap Value	GTIIX	Glenmede Philadelphia International
Intl Small Cap	LZSMX	Lazard Intl Small Cap Open
Intl Small Cap Value		*not available*
Emerging Markets	LZOEX	Lazard Emerging Markets Open

TABLE 33.3   FIDELITY PORTFOLIO

Short Term Bond	FSHBX	Fidelity Short-term Bond
Intermediate Term Bond	FTBFX	Fidelity Total Bond
Commodities	PCRDX	PIMCO Commodity Real Return Strategy D
Real Estate	FRESX	Fidelity Real Estate Investment Portfolio
US Large Cap	FSMKX	Fidelity Spartan 500 Index
US Large Cap Value	FSLVX	Fidelity Structured Large Cap Value
US Small Cap	FSLCX	Fidelity Small Cap Stock
US Small Cap Value	FCPVX	Fidelity Small Cap Value
Intl Large Cap	FSIIX	Fidelity Spartan International Index
Intl Large Cap Value	FIVLX	Fidelity International Value
Intl Small Cap	FSCOX	Fidelity Intl Small Cap Opportunity
Intl Small Cap Value		*not available*
Emerging Markets	FEMKX	Fidelity Emerging Markets

TABLE 33.4   T. ROWE PRICE PORTFOLIO

Short Term Bond	PRWBX	T. Rowe Price Short Term Bond
Intermediate Term Bond	PBDIX	T. Rowe Price US Bond Index
Commodities	PRNEX	T. Rowe Price New Era Fund (**not** a commodities index fund)
Real Estate	TRREX	T. Rowe Price Real Estate
US Large Cap	PREIX	T. Rowe Price Equity Index 500
US Large Cap Value	TRVLX	T. Rowe Price Value
US Small Cap	PRDSX	T. Rowe Price Diversified Small Cap
US Small Cap Value	PRSVX	T. Rowe Price Small Cap Value
Intl Large Cap	PIEQX	T. Rowe Price International Equity Index
Intl Large Cap Value	TRIGX	T. Rowe Price International Growth & Income
Intl Small Cap	PRIDX	T. Rowe Price International Discovery
Intl Small Cap Value		*not available*
Emerging Markets	PRMSX	T. Rowe Price Emerging Markets

Care must be taken to assure that the index used is the best available. No one outside of DFA has an international small cap value index fund. Outside of DFA, Vanguard remains the leader in index coverage, but still has no International small and International small value.

Chapter 34
Working with a Financial Advisor

Abstract -   Work only with a fee-only-advisor who understands modern portfolio theory and is committed to asset class index fund investing.

How can you get good, unbiased advice? The answer is really fairly simple. **First**, use a fee-only-advisor. **Second**, assure yourself that your advisor understands Modern Portfolio Theory.

Fee-only-advisor. Work only with financial advisors who earn their income from their advice and financial planning services. Do not work with commission-based advisors (they have a natural bias toward investment products and strategies that earn them commissions rather than earn returns for you). This conflict of interest is unnecessary – find a fee-only-advisor. Even with a fee-only-advisor, always be clear about any additional commissions on the "products" they are recommending to you. Ask explicitly.

You can expect fees to range from 0.5% to 1.25% of your nestegg (assets under management) per year. If your nestegg is less than $500,000 you will be at the high end of the range. If your nestegg is over $1,000,000 you should be able to negotiate a fee toward the low end of the range. Some advisors, such as Evanson Asset Management, offer a very low flat annual fee for Modern Portfolio management (providing the limited management required for passive asset class investing). Most people will find this bare bones approach too weak and will benefit from a more traditional and personal relationship with an investment advisor.

You should always use a large well-known brokerage firm, such as Fidelity, Schwab, Vanguard, TD Ameritrade or Jack White, to hold your nestegg assets. Be sure that their statements are mailed directly to you. You will need to execute a limited power of attorney to allow your advisor to trade on your account. Be sure it does not allow your advisor the right to withdraw funds from your account.

Modern Portfolio Theory. Confirm that your advisor understands Modern Portfolio Theory and is committed to its tenets. Be aware that many advisors claim to believe in Modern Portfolio Theory but are still involved in active management. If your advisor is recommending individual stocks, trying to time exposure to and withdrawal from the market, or chasing recent high performance by funds or money managers, he is practicing active management. If he believes that you can regularly beat the benchmarks, he is not convinced that the market is efficient. Trying to "beat the benchmark" should be a warning to you. You want to track the benchmark, not beat it.

If a fund or manager appears to have beaten a benchmark for several years, ask about the benchmark. Comparing a manager to the wrong benchmark could make him look like the next Warren Buffet. For example, you should always ask to see a value manager compared to an appropriate value benchmark. Compare each fund or money manager to the most appropriate available benchmark.

Chapter 35

Rebalancing

Abstract - Don't rebalance too frequently – once a year is enough. The concept is simple, just try to maintain your original asset allocation percentages through time. Rebalancing will increase your return by causing you to sell high and buy low.

A Modern Portfolio Theory portfolio does not behave like the rest of the market. There will be times when you will be very far out of step with the news reports about the market (the "Dow", the NASDAQ and the S&P 500). From my experience, these are trying times. Like the period from 1995 through 1999 when the S&P 500 outperformed everything. I was underperforming the "market", with an average return across those years of around 15% when the S&P 500 averaged over 28%. But then there's the flip side, like 2000 through 2002. Those times were kind of fun, with all the puzzled looks from friends and associates who were losing their shirts in those years and asking me **"How can you be UP in a market like this?"**. This phenomenon is called "tracking error" by academics. Whatever you chose to call it, get used to it. You have intentionally included asset classes in your portfolio that are poorly correlated with the market. In the long run you will benefit, but in the short run you will just have to smile, rain or shine.

The concept of rebalancing is simple. You just try to maintain your original asset allocation percentages through time. The idea of rebalancing may even sound benign, but you will probably have to **force** yourself to put your hard earned money into an asset class that looks like a dog (like value funds during that S&P 500 run in the late 90's). You may even question the wisdom of something so counterintuitive. But if you persevere, you will establish the discipline of buying low and selling high. Eventually it will even be fun to have such "bargains" available.

Over time you will find yourself paying less and less attention to the day-to-day or month-to-month noise in the market and relax. The confidence of knowing that long term, you will do about as well as it is possible to do (without 'gambling') is very reassuring. Somewhere down the road you may even stop worrying about your investments at all. You will sleep well.

The rebalancing required in your nestegg will only take a few hours at the end of each year. Your strategies will be different before and after retirement.

In the accumulation phase:

You should add any new investment money first to funds that have done poorly. If this alone does not bring the portfolio back into its asset allocation balance, you may need to transfer some from the high performers to add to the funds with the worst returns. This discipline will cause YOU to sell high and buy low (while most others are panicking and selling low and then buying high by chasing the high flyers which don't usually continue up).

During retirement:

In bad years, withdraw only from fixed income (to allow the equity funds to recover).
In good years, withdraw first from the top performing equity funds, then second from all funds pro-rata to maintain allocation. (see Chapters 39 and 40)

Don't bother trying to get all the funds exactly on their allocation percentages. A good rule of thumb is to keep percentages within 5% of their targets (e.g. 65% equities back to 60%). Don't rebalance too frequently – once a year (or even every two years) is enough. In addition to reducing return, the tax impact of overly aggressive rebalancing can become significant.

Chapter 36
Investment Policy

Abstract - Most investors benefit from spelling out their investment policy in writing and in detail. The only time your investment policy should change is in response to significant life changes in your financial condition, objectives or time horizons.

Write it down, then stick to it.

An Investment Policy should include your goals, objectives and strategies for:

1. **Cash reserves** – say 6 months normal spending

2. **General goals and objectives** – regarding saving for a house, kids' college, retirement, etc. (money for very short term goals should be shifted into cash reserves)

3. **Time Horizon**

4. **Risk** (maximum loss you are willing to accept in any one year)

5. **Asset Classes** (and target allocations to be in portfolio)
   a. Fixed Income
   b. Large Cap
   c. Small Cap
   d. Value
   e. International
   f. Emerging Markets
   g. REITs and commodities

6. **Rebalancing strategy**

7. **Withdrawal strategy** (in retirement)

The only time your investment policy should change is in response to significant life changes in your financial condition, objectives or time horizon. Otherwise, stay the course.

> *"History teaches that both investment managers and clients need help if they are to hold successfully to the discipline of long-term commitments. This means restraining themselves from reacting to disconcerting short-term data and keeping themselves from taking those unwise actions that seem so 'obvious' and urgent to optimists at market highs and pessimists at market lows. In short, policy is the most powerful antidote to panic."*

> *"For investors, the real opportunity to achieve superior results is not in scrambling to outperform the market, but in establishing and adhering to appropriate investment policies over the long term – policies that position the portfolio to benefit from riding with the main long term forces of the market."*

> Charles Ellis, The Loser's Game, p 23, 60

Part Five

Retirement

Chapter 37

Retirement Calculators and Withdrawal Strategies

Abstract - Beware of retirement calculators – many of them overstate the amount you can safely withdraw from your nestegg in retirement. On the other hand some are so conservative that they will have you living like a pauper while your money piles up for your heirs. Only calculators based on modern portfolios and Monte Carlo analysis will reflect "safe" withdrawal rates accurately.

Beware of overly simplistic retirement calculators. Overconfidence in high returns and low deviation from averages can cause high withdrawals that cannot be supported through the market downturns we should reasonably expect. For example, just because you expect 11% returns with 3% inflation does not mean you can withdraw the 8% difference every year. Your nestegg will be decimated if the market declines by 25% or 30% for a few years, which you should expect to happen sometime during your life. If it happens in your first year of retirement, it would be very bad news. If you continued high withdrawals, your nestegg would not recover and you would run out of money! Most reputable financial planners have abandoned the "linear" calculators that produced those absurdly high withdrawals.

I have seen retirement calculators that recommend everything from 3% of nestegg to 8% of nestegg withdrawal rates (even more for older retirees), and of course there's the old 5% rule used by bank trust departments over the years. Recently there have been a handful of careful academic studies that argue for very small withdrawals (in the 3% to 5% range).

Perhaps most notable among these has come to be known as *the Trinity Study"* published in 1997 by Phillip L. Cooley, Carl M. Hubbard and Daniel T. Walz, three faculty members of Trinity University. Their back-testing study looked at the periods from 1926 to 1995. They used the returns from a portfolio consisting of only the S&P 500 and long-term high-grade corporate bonds. They concluded that only a withdrawal rate of from 4% to 5% of the initial portfolio value (e.g. $40,000 or $50,000 from a $1,000,000 portfolio) had a reasonable expectation of success. Cooley, Hubbard and Walz reconfirmed their study in 2003.

William Bernstein published his *Retirement Calculator from Hell* in 1998. He makes the point that even 4% or 5% can be disastrous if you retire just before the next market collapse. In his *Retirement Calculator from Hell – Part II and Part III* (both published in 2001) he shares more gloom. You should read all of these if you're feeling cocky about very high withdrawal rates. Stuff happens – really (you can find them at *www.efficientfrontier.com*).

The scary withdrawal rate studies have an important flaw in common, they are all based on portfolios dominated by the S&P 500 (and therefore having lower returns and higher volatility than the modern portfolios in the previous section). Volatility is crucial.

Monte Carlo analysis reveals the clear link between lower volatility and higher withdrawal safety for all time horizons. Monte Carlo analysis, developed in the Manhattan Project in the 1940's, as applied to retirement finance, involves the generation of random draws of numbers based on the return and standard deviation of a given portfolio and the analysis of thousands of potential future scenarios including withdrawal strategies.

Volatility skews withdrawal results. The median return is less than the (mean) average. This means that at a given withdrawal rate more people go broke than get rich even though the average result is the same. A very small number of players obtain very much higher than expected results, while a large number of players either fail or obtain lower than expected results. The relative safety of various potential withdrawal rates is a hotly debated issue.

As demonstrated in the previous section, a modern portfolio will typically have more than a 2% additional return with lower risk. This additional return (and lower risk) should increase the potential "safe" withdrawal rate from a modern portfolio. New studies using modern portfolios and Monte Carlo analysis confirm this.

Frank Armstrong, in a November 2005 article in the CPA Journal, *Measuring Volatility and the Cost of Retirement,* points out these problems in the 90's studies by the Trinity professors. Armstrong redoes the analysis using portfolios with 10%, 15% and 20% standard deviations. Using a 6% withdrawal rate, he finds that 23% of portfolios with a 20% standard deviation fail at 30years; 10% of portfolios with a standard deviation of 15% fail; but only 1% of portfolios with a standard deviation of 10% fail. This is of extraordinary importance because a modern portfolio achieves around the 10% standard deviation.

In addition, research is beginning to show that spending does not stay high across the whole retirement life cycle. Several studies have shown that we will spend less as we get older. Kenn Tacchino and Cynthia Saltzman, *Do Accumulation Models Over-state What's Needed to Retire?*, Journal of Financial Planning, Feb 1999, find that "the downward adjustment in spending by age 75 is approximately 20% of the initial spending levels during retirement that starts at age 65."

Similarly, Ty Bernike, *Reality Retirement Planning: A New Paradigm for an Old Science*, Journal of Financial Planning, June 2005, confirms that real spending will decrease incrementally throughout retirement. Both of these studies find that the inevitable increase in health care spending is usually smaller than the decrease in other spending in our later years.

More research is needed to confirm safe withdrawal rates from modern portfolios, but the upward pressure from the increased return, the decreased risk of modern portfolios and the decreased spending in older years are likely to produce marginally higher safe withdrawal rates. The danger of a string of very bad years in early retirement is a potential retirement catastrophe. Being conservative in the early years of retirement will greatly increase the chances that your nestegg will grow comfortably. Being aggressive in the early years of retirement can cause you to run out of money.

Some argue for 85% safety as a withdrawal rate goal; others for 90%; others for 95%; and a few argue for 99% safety. You need to get a feel for what these mean. The relationship of safety, failure and average nestegg growth can be seen in the following data for a $1,000,000 nestegg:

Safety	Failure Rate	Withdrawal Rate	Withdrawal Amount	Average Nestegg after 35 years today's dollars
85%	15%	5.3%	$53,000	$1,167,000
95%	5%	4.7%	$47,000	$1,797,000
99%	1%	4.0%	$40,000	$2,385,000

You can see above that the increasing safety (by decreasing withdrawal rate) increases the likelihood that your nestegg will grow quite large. Most financial advisors aim at 85% safety (the large nestegg required for more safety is a difficult goal for many). I think 95% safety is a good goal (but I entered retirement with an 85% safe withdrawal rate required), a little consulting for three years allowed my nestegg to grow to where I can now use a 95% safe withdrawal rate. I am 99% safe with the withdrawals required for my "Turtle Budget."

Chapter 38
Sleep Well Withdrawal Strategies

Abstract – Keep at least 25% in fixed income assets to provide for several years of normal expenses. This rainy day fund will allow you to sleep well. Withdrawal rates are provided for a modern portfolio at 85%, 95% and 99% safety.

In order to sleep well, with money in the stock market, most of us need a rainy day fund. With four, five, or maybe even six years of normal expenses in fixed income assets, most people will have a better chance of avoiding a panic reaction in one of the nasty stock market "collapses" that are sure to come. The basic idea is simple: in the good stock market years withdraw whatever did best (to rebalance); in the bad stock market years withdraw from fixed income assets (to allow the stock funds to recover).

A 95% safe withdrawal rate is a very good goal (very few can afford to limit themselves to the withdrawal rate required for 99% safety). An 85% safe withdrawal rate is ok, maybe even good; but it may require you to be flexible in retirement (maybe reducing expenses from time to time or working part-time a little). If you're planning some consulting work or a second career of some kind this may fit well. With your "turtle budget," 99% safety should be your goal.

Withdrawal rates for 85%, 95% and 99% safety are shown below for a range of retirement periods. As you can see, you can withdraw a little more as you get older.

FIGURE 38.1   SAFE WITHDRAWAL RATES FROM MODERN PORTFOLIOS

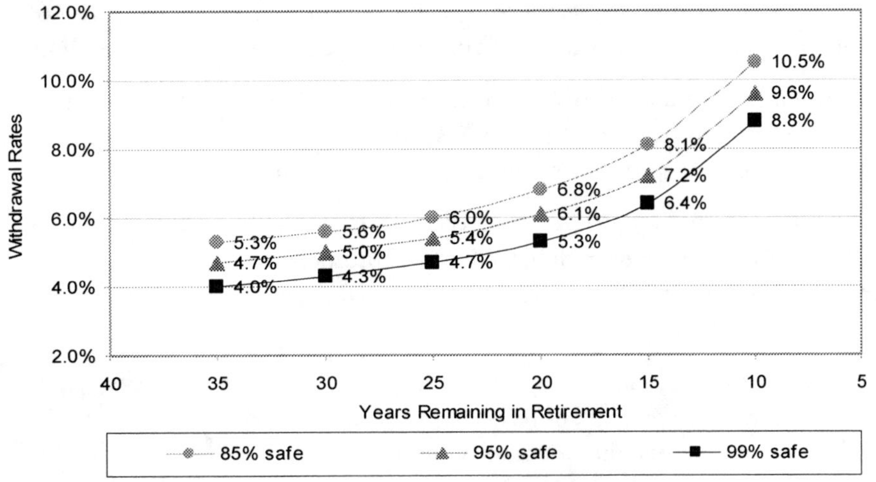

Caveat: If your nestegg collapses by 25% or more in the first 5 years of your retirement, try to shift to the 99% withdrawal rate curve. Turn "turtle", pull back in your shell, reduce expenses, make sure you can ride it out. If you can't make it to the 99% curve, at least reduce expenses (and withdrawals) as much as you can.

You can review things every 3 to 5 years. If your nestegg has grown large you could leave your initial inflation adjusted withdrawal amount as is and allow your safety to increase; or recalibrate by adjusting your withdrawal to a new higher initial withdrawal amount at the original safety level; or withdraw a large chunk of your nestegg for a special purchase like a second home or charitable gift (leaving a nestegg that provides withdrawals at the level you want). If your nestegg has not grown (at least a little) you may want to adjust your withdrawal rate down.

Chapter 39

Boomers and Social Security
Will It be there for Us?

Abstract -   Social Security will probably be there for all boomers. But the benefits may be marginally lower. The normal retirement age will probably increase again; and the early retirement age may be increased.

The Social Security Act of 1935 provides (a little) guaranteed retirement money for all.

Social Security's reserves began accumulating in 1977. It continues today to take in more than it is paying out – the "reserve" (the excess) is being held in government bonds. The bean counters at Social Security project they will continue to be able to pay benefits solely from current revenue until 2016. From 2017 to 2026, Social Security will have to draw more heavily from the interest on their government bonds. After 2026, Social Security will need to start cashing in those bonds, which will run out in 2038. After 2038, the bean counters project that there will only be enough revenue from taxes to pay 72% of benefits.

The normal retirement age (NRA) was established by the original Social Security Act at 65; and the NRA remained 65 until it was changed in 1983. This change was partly in response to the looming demographic problem of 80 million retiring baby boomers, and partly in response to the simple fact that life expectancy had changed dramatically. At the turn of the century (1900) the average life expectancy was only 46 years. Today it is over 70 years.

In 1983, Congress increased the Normal Retirement Age for boomers from 65 to from 66 to 67, depending on when you were born. So far the early retirement age (currently 62) is unchanged.

The Baby Boomers are the large number of people born between 1946 and 1964; the peak birth year was 1954. The 1946 cohort will reach 66 (their NRA) in 2012; the 1964 cohort will reach age 67 (their NRA) in 2031. This group of over 80 million will overwhelm the current system.

When the reserves are exhausted, in 2038, there are choices to be made (hopefully Congress will be clever enough to address this issue before then). There are numerous proposals on how to close the gap. It's anyone's guess what will eventually be done, but the following things are being discussed:

1.   Increasing the current payroll tax
2.   Increasing the maximum wage subject to Social Security tax
3.   Taxing Social Security benefits like pension benefits
4.   Including new state and government workers
5.   Additional increases to the Normal Retirement Age
6.   Moving the early retirement age from 62 to 63 (or higher)
7.   Cutting benefits (future benefits have already been cut by changing the inflation adjustment from wage to price inflation)
8.   Investing some of the trust fund in private securities
9.   Creating personal Social Security retirement accounts (privatization)

Some Social Security will be there. But benefits may be marginally lower (probably not more than 10% lower), the Normal Retirement Age will likely increase again (maybe by one year), and the early retirement age may be increased (again maybe by one year). Whatever finally gets done, it seems likely that we will all get something, eventually.

Chapter 40
Social Security Benefits

Abstract - Social Security benefits vary significantly based on your earnings and the age you retire.

The easiest (and most accurate) way to determine the amount of your estimated benefits is to look at the *Social Security Statement* you recently started receiving each year from the Social Security Administration. If you misplaced this statement (or did not yet receive one) you can request one by calling 800-772-1213 or by writing to Social Security Administration, Office of Earnings Operations, P.O. Box 33026, Baltimore, MD 21290-3026. Additional information can also be found by visiting *www.ssa.gov*.

The amount you would get at your normal retirement age is your Primary Insurance Amount. To qualify for benefits you must have earned 40 work credits, generally equal to about 10 years of earnings. For people born after 1928, Social Security counts your 35 years of highest earnings after 1950 (or age 21 whichever is later) to determine your benefits. For earnings before age 60, your earnings are adjusted upward by an inflation factor for each year. Earnings after age 60 are not indexed. The average of your 35 highest yearly earnings is used to determine your benefit. The Average Indexed Monthly Earnings (AIME) is used to calculate your benefits.

The formula used has three parts, creating bend points in benefits, favoring lower income workers.

The first $656 of AIME is multiplied by **90%**;
The next $3,299 of AIME (up to $3,955) is multiplied by **32%**; and
All AIME over $3,955 is multiplied by **15%**.

The following example uses three hypothetical workers all age 62 in 2001: one with average earnings; one with high earnings; one with maximum Social Security earnings.

TABLE 40.1   PIA FOR THREE HYPOTHETICAL WORKERS

	AVERAGE (A)	HIGH (B)	MAXIMUM (C)
Current Salary	$35,000	$55,000	$90,000
Total Indexed Earnings (35 yrs)	$1,244,491	$1,958,625	$2,726.531
Average Indexed Monthly Earnings	2,963	4,663	6,492
90% of first $656	590.40	590.40	590.40
32% to $3,955	738.26	1055.68	1055.68
15% over $3,955	0.00	106.26	380.51
Primary Insurance Amount (PIA)	1,328.66	1,752.34	2,026.59
PIA (rounded down to 0.10)	$1,328.60	$1,752.30	$2,026.50

If you are married, your spouse will receive 50% of your amount. So your benefit, if married, is at least 150% of your personal benefit amount (possibly more if your spouse has earnings too). The survivor benefit for your spouse is 100% of your benefit amount at age 65; but only 71.5% at age 60 (100% minus 0.475% per month before age 65 that the benefit is elected).

Early Retirement (age 62)

The formula for the reduction in benefits for early retirement (age 62) is a little complicated. The benefit is reduced by 5/9 of one percent for each month before your normal retirement age (up to 36 months), and then 5/12 of one percent for each month over three years before normal retirement age.

> If you retire at 62 with a normal retirement age of 66:
> 36 months @ 5/9 = 20%
> 12 months @ 5/12 = 5%
> total reduction for **4 years** early therefore = **25%**
>
> If you retire at 62 with a normal retirement age of 67:
> 36 months @ 5/9 = 20%
> 24 months @ 5/12 = 10%
> total reduction for **5 years** early therefore = **30%**

If you chose to retire early and elect to receive benefits early, your benefits will be permanently reduced based on these factors. Most people who retire very early choose to take their Social Security at age 62. It will take you about 17 years (of the higher age 65 payments) to overcome the benefit of receiving the lower payment from age 62.

Delayed Retirement (up to age 70)

The formula for the increase in benefits for delayed retirement is less complicated. The benefit is increased for each year worked after your normal retirement age (up to age 70) by the applicable percentage from the following table.

Year of birth	Increase in Benefits per year of delayed retirement
1924 or before	3.0%
1925, 1926	3.5%
1927, 1928	4.0%
1929, 1930	4.5%
1931, 1932	5.0%
1933, 1934	5.5%
1935, 1936	6.0%
1937, 1938	6.5%
1939, 1940	7.0%
1941, 1942	7.5%
1943 or later	8.0%

Therefore all boomers (1946-1964) will have their benefits increased by 8.0% for each year worked after their normal retirement age. Since boomers' normal retirement age ranges from 66 to 67; their maximum increase in benefits ranges from 24% (3 x 8% with NRA of 67) to 32% (4 x 8% with NRA of 66).

Very Early Retirement (before age 62)

What about retirement earlier than 62, say at 58, or 55 (or even earlier)?

The impact of retirement before the age of 62 is not discussed in "Your Social Security Statement". It is also not discussed in most retirement guide books. Very early retirement will further decrease your Social Security benefits, but depending on your earnings history the impact may be smaller than you might have expected.

The impact in your individual case depends on how many years with no earnings are included in your 35 years of highest earnings. If you retire at age 57 (and have only the 5 years from age 57 to 62 with no earnings) your PIA will not be reduced at all. If you retire at age 55, you will have at least 2 years with no earnings.

The following example is based on retirement at age 55 with no earnings from age 55 to age 62. Building on the hypothetical example above we can substitute average earnings for all three workers in the years from 22 to 27 (to reflect the fact that high or maximum earnings in those years are very rare), and zero in the years from 55 to 62 (to reflect very early retirement). The following changes in AIME and PIA result:

TABLE 40.2   PIA FOR RETIREMENT AT 55

	AVERAGE (A)	HIGH (B)	MAXIMUM (C)
Working to age **62** from above:			
Total Indexed Earnings (35 yrs)	$1,244,491	$1,958,625	$2,726,531
Average Indexed Monthly Earnings	2,693	4,663	6,492
PIA (rounded down to 0.10)	$1,328.60	$1,752.30	$2,026.50
Retiring at **55**:			
Total Indexed Earnings (35 yrs)	$1,176,415	$1,779,641	$2,324,240
Average Indexed Monthly Earnings	2,801	4,237	5,534
PIA (rounded down to 0.10)	$1,276.80	$1,688.40	$1,882.90
Reduction in monthly PIA from retiring at 55	$51.80	$63.90	$143.60

The reduction in PIA is far smaller than might be expected from seven years of zero earnings between 55 and 62. The actual benefit at age 62 will be from 70% to 75% of your PIA (depending on your normal retirement age) – discussed above. The real show stopper for early retirement isn't Social Security, it's health insurance – discussed in the next chapter.

Summary of Social Benefits

By applying the various formulas for delayed, early or very early retirement we can arrive at a rough estimate of Social Security benefits at 55, 62, 65 and 70 for these hypothetical workers.

TABLE 40.3   SOCIAL SECURITY BENEFITS

	AVERAGE (A) $35,000		HIGH (B) $55,000		MAXIMUM (C) over $90,000	
Earnings						
Benefits per:	mo	year	mo	year	mo	year
Retire at **55**	$925	$11,110	$1,224	$14,690	$1,365	$16,380
Retire at **62**	963	11,560	1,270	15,245	1,469	17,630
Retire at **65**	1,329	15,945	1,752	21,030	2,027	24,320
Retire at **70**	1,700	20,410	2,243	26,915	2,595	31,130

Note: These numbers are very rough estimates and should not be used for detailed planning. Your date of birth, earnings history, date of retirement, and choice of when to start receiving benefits will determine your exact benefit amount. In addition, you should expect some changes in the Social Security system (none of the changes being considered will increase your benefit).

For more information, check out   www.socialsecuritybenefitshandbook.com

The next chapter discusses health insurance in early retirement.

Chapter 41

Health Insurance in Early Retirement
Before Medicare Eligibility

Abstract - If you retire before you are eligible for Medicare (currently age 65) you will need health insurance coverage from some other source.

If you don't have health insurance, you may not be able to retire before age 65. Without insurance, a serious illness, even if you recover fully, can wipe you out financially. If you retire before you are eligible for Medicare (currently age 65) you need health insurance coverage from some other source. There are really only five choices.

1. Continuing Employer-Sponsored health coverage (very rare and getting rarer!)
2. COBRA Coverage (maximum of 18 months)
3. Private Individual Health Insurance
4. Special Group Health Insurance (small employer or professional groups)
5. State High Risk Insurance Pool (very expensive, not in every State)

Continuing Employer-Sponsored Health Insurance

Those of you who have an early retirement option with your employer are lucky – not many of us do. And employers that have such plans are desperate to get out of them because they are so expensive. In the future this option is going to become even more rare. If your company does offer early retirement health care insurance as a benefit, you need to confirm the eligibility, tenure, premiums, coverages and lifetime caps – they could vary significantly from your situation while still working.

COBRA coverage

If you have only a short time until you are eligible for Medicare (less than 18 months), you can elect to purchase coverage under COBRA, the Consolidated Omnibus Budget Reconciliation Act. By law you are charged 102% of the group rate. COBRA offers you additional benefits under the HIPAA (the Kennedy-Kassebaum Act – the Health Insurance Portability and Accountability Act of 1996). Several states require that insurance companies that sell individual plans must offer them to individuals that qualify under HIPAA. The premiums may be prohibitive, but the coverage is available.

Private Individual Health Insurance Coverage

If you don't have access to group coverage, and do not have medical problems, you may be able to buy individual health insurance. The premiums for individual policies are based on your age, your medical history, deductibles, co-payments and lifetime caps. At least one of the following five insurance companies offers individual insurance in your state:

American Family Insurance	*www.american-family.com* (15 states)
Blue Cross Blue Shield	*www.bcbs.com* (all 50 states)
Fortis Health	*www.fortishealth.com*
Golden Rule Insurance	*www.goldenrule.com* (all states except NY)
Trustmark Insurance	*www.trustmarkinsurance.com*

As a rule **you cannot get individual health insurance if you are in poor health**. If you have a poor medical history, they will almost always consider you a bad risk and refuse to offer you coverage, or alternatively under certain conditions they may offer you coverage only if you sign a waiver that excludes coverage for certain pre-existing conditions.

The most important variables in individual health insurance are the following:

1   **Maximum Benefit Limit** – the lifetime maximum that the policy will pay per covered person. You want at least $2,000,000 (preferably $3,000,000, if you can find it).

2   **Coinsurance Amount** – the amount of covered expenses shared on some basis like 80/20 between the insurance company and you. You will typically pay 20% of the first $10,000 or $15,000 of total medical expenses after your deductible (a total co-pay of about $2,000 to $3,000 maximum). Many policies have no coinsurance (paying 100% of expenses after the deductible is met). These policies have higher premiums but lower maximum out-of-pocket expense.

3   **Deductible** – the total amount each insured person must pay for covered expenses before the insurance kicks in. Deductibles typically range from $500 to as much as $5,000 (or $10,000 for husband and wife family policies). Tax deductible Health Savings Accounts (HSA) are available with certain policies with very high deductibles.

4   **Maximum Out-of-pocket Expense in a Policy Year** – the maximum combination of coinsurance and deductible expenses (in addition to your premium) you might pay in any one year. For an **individual** the amount will be the deductible plus about $2,000 coinsurance. For a **couple** the amount will be two times the deductible plus the $2,000 coinsurance. Your maximum total expense will be your premium plus the maximum out-of-pocket expenses.

Costs for individual coverage can vary extremely widely. Some policies have prescription coverage, most do not. Some exclude coverage abroad. Higher deductibles can lower rates dramatically – but still provide adequate catastrophic coverage. The annual premium increases with age by about 5%. Inflation and other annual cost increases can vary extremely widely. Representative costs for individual health insurance policies for males of the indicated age are shown in the table below. Females are about 20% less than males. A family premium (for husband and wife together) is only about 15% more than the male alone.

TABLE 41.1   INDIVIDUAL HEALTH CARE ANNUAL INSURANCE PREMIUMS

Deductible	age 55	age 58	age 62	age 64
$500	$7,000	$8,000	$9,500	$10,500
$1,000	$5,000	$6,000	$7,300	$8,000
$1,500	$4,000	$4,500	$5,500	$6,000
$2,500	$3,300	$3,800	$4,500	$5,000
$5,000	$2,800	$3,200	$3,800	$4,000

Premiums can be lowered by about 20% if you elect coverage with a 20% coinsurance payment for all costs through about $15,000 (lowering your premium, but raising your maximum out-of-pocket).

If you plan on moving you need to confirm that your coverage is portable. Research your options carefully. You don't want to need to change companies after you develop a medical condition that would preclude obtaining coverage from another company.

The office of the State Insurance Commissioner in many states offers Consumers' Guides to buying private individual insurance. You should contact your state's commissioner for any advice the office is willing to give, such as additional companies offering individual insurance.

Several states have enacted either "guaranteed issue" laws or "community rating" systems. Guaranteed issue laws require insurance companies to provide insurance to individuals regardless of their health condition. Community rating systems require insurance companies to charge everyone the same premium regardless of health condition. Some even require the same premium regardless of age as well.

The result has been dramatically higher premiums in many of these states with far fewer choices for individuals. The worst states include: Kentucky, Maine, New Jersey, New York, Vermont and Washington state. States with no "guaranteed issue" laws or "community rating" systems (and therefore more competitive insurance) include: Alabama, Alaska, Arizona, Arkansas, California, Colorado, Connecticut, Delaware, Florida, Georgia, Illinois, Kansas, Maryland, Mississippi, Missouri, Montana, Nebraska, Nevada, North Carolina, Tennessee and Texas. The remainder of the states fall in between.

Special Group Health Insurance

There are a handful of mainly professional organizations that offer group health insurance to their members. These groups are not as common or generally available as you might have been led to believe. Most of the ads you see for group insurance available to individuals is really individual health insurance. Good insurance companies have no interest in underwriting groups that solicit hard to insure individuals that masquerade as a group. The exception to this rule is in states with "guaranteed issue" laws or "community rating" systems. In these states, forming a small employer group can sidestep the onerous rules for individual coverage and allow more competitive insurance.

State High Risk Insurance Pool

Thirty states currently have high risk insurance pools that are required to provide coverage to individuals who cannot get private individual health coverage because of health problems – pre-existing medical conditions. Generally, you must have exhausted all COBRA rights and been refused private individual coverage. You must also not be eligible for Medicaid.

The cost is significantly higher than private individual insurance but is capped in most states at some percentage over the average premium for private individual coverage. States with high risk insurance pools include:

State	Phone	State	Phone
Alabama	877 619 2447	Missouri	800 821 2231
Alaska	888 290 0616	Montana	406 444 8263
Arkansas	501 378 2979	Nebraska	800 356 3485
California	800 289 6574	New Hampshire	603 227 7265
Colorado	800 511 5774	New Mexico	800 432 0750
Connecticut	800 842 0004	North Dakota	800 737 0016
Florida	850 309 1200	Oklahoma	913 362 0040
Illinois	800 367 6410	Oregon	800 542 3104
Indiana	800 552 7921	South Carolina	800 868 2500
Iowa	800 877 5156	South Dakota	web site
Kansas	800 290 1368	Tennessee	615 741 0177
Kentucky	317 614 2000	Texas	888 398 3927
Louisiana	800 532 5274	Utah	866 880 8494
Maryland	866 780 7105	Washington	800 877 5187
Minnesota	952 593 9609	Wisconsin	800 828 4777
Mississippi	888 820 9400	Wyoming	307 634 1393

Call your State Insurance Commissioner to determine local conditions. Even if you can only find very expensive coverage, you should probably still consider it. Most of us cannot afford to self-insure for $2,000,000 in medical expenses.

Chapter 42
Medicare, Medigap and Long Term Care Insurance

Abstract - Even if you couldn't get health insurance before then, you will have it at age 65 with Medicare. But there are 'gaps' in the coverage that can be filled with Medigap insurance. Long term care insurance is expensive but needs to be considered.

The Medicare-Medicaid bill of 1965 amended the Social Security Act and established Medicare. Starting at age 65, the federal government will pay a lot of your medical bills. Even if you couldn't get health insurance before then, you will have it age 65. It has saved a lot of seniors from having their life savings wiped out by medical bills. But Medicare doesn't pay **all** of your medical bills. There are gaps in the coverage – hence Medigap insurance. And there are a lot of complicated options. The figures below are for 2006.

Medicare Part A

Medicare Part A is the basic **hospitalization insurance** you are automatically entitled to when you reach age 65. There is **no premium to pay – it is free**. It mainly covers inpatient hospital stays, but also covers some skilled nursing care after a hospital visit, and home health care or hospice care under some circumstances.

Medicare currently pays for the first 60 days of hospitalization in full, except for a $952 deductible (for each "benefit period'). For days 61-90, you are responsible for a co-pay $238 per day. For days 91-150 (60 lifetime reserve days you can use only once), you have a co-pay of $476 per day. After that you're on your own – that's a big gap! Make sure you fill it.

TABLE 42.1   MEDICARE PART A HOSPITALIZATION COVERAGE

	Deductible or co-pay
First 60 days of hospitalization	a $952 per period deductible
Days 61 to 90	a $238 per day co-payment
Days 91 to 150	a $476 per day co-payment
After day 150	100% (no Medicare coverage at all)

You start over (new "benefit period") after you have been out of the hospital for 60 days.

The coverage for skilled nursing care is limited to 100 days; days 1-20 are fully covered, days 21-100 require a co-pay of $119.00 per day. After that you're on your own. Medicare is not long term care insurance.

TABLE 42.2   MEDICARE PART A SKILLED NURSING CARE COVERAGE

	Deductible or co-pay
First 20 days of hospitalization	$0 (fully covered)
Days 21 to 100	a $119.00 per day co-payment
After day 100	100% (no Medicare coverage at all)

Medicare Part B

Medicare Part B covers doctor's services, lab tests, outpatient hospital services, durable medical equipment and certain other services not covered by Medicare Part A. This **optional supplementary insurance** has a **premium of $88.50** per month. There is a $124 per year deductible and a co-pay of 20%. This is a great buy.

Medicare Part A and Part B are a good foundation on which to build good medical coverage; but without additional coverage, you are still exposed to potentially ruinous medical expenses and have limited your options for obtaining the care you will want.

Medicare Part C and Medigap Insurance

Medicare Part C (Medicare+Choice; now Medicare Advantage) was created by the Balanced Budget Act of 1997. This is more or less federal Medigap coverage, but it requires you to use specific doctors, hospitals and services to have your expenses covered. Premiums vary with age and states. Since the passage of the Medicare Prescription Drug, Improvement, and Modernization Act of 2003, Medicare+Choice became known as Medicare Advantage (MA) plans. In addition to offering comparable coverage to Part A and Part B, Medicare Advantage plans may also offer Part D (Prescription Drug) coverage. You cannot have both Part C and private Medigap insurance. Most of you will choose private Medigap insurance.

Medigap insurance is private supplemental insurance meant to close the gaps in coverage left by Medicare Part A and Part B. It is complicated. So complicated (and subject to abuse) that in 1992 Congress required all states to standardize Medigap plans. There are now 10 basic types of Medigap policies which are standard in all states (except Massachusetts, Minnesota and Wisconsin which each has its own standard). Because the coverage is standardized, you can shop for the best price from the highest quality company. The following table summarizes the 10 Medigap Plans:

Plans	A	B	C	D	E	F	G	H	I	J	K	L
Core Benefits												
Part A Hospital (days 61-90)	x	x	x	x	x	x	x	x	x	x	x	x
Lifetime Reserve (days 91-150)	x	x	x	x	x	x	x	x	x	x	x	x
365 Life Hospital Days	x	x	x	x	x	x	x	x	x	x	x	x
Part A & B Blood	x	x	x	x	x	x	x	x	x	x	50%	75%
Part B 20% Coinsurance	x	x	x	x	x	x	x	x	x	x	50%	75%
Additional Benefits												
Part A Hospital Deductible		x	x	x	x	x	x	x	x	x	50%	75%
Skilled Nursing Facility Coinsurance			x	x	x	x	x	x	x	x	50%	75%
Foreign Travel Emergency			x	x	x	x	x	x	x	x		
Part B Deductible			x			x				x		
At-home Recovery				x			x		x	x		
Part B Excess Doctor Charges						100%	80%		100%	100%		
Preventive Care and Screening					x					x		

Plans A through J have the same basic coverage and tend to have higher premiums with lower (or no) out-of-pocket costs; plans K and L have different basic coverage and tend to have lower premiums with higher out-of-pocket costs (plan K has a $4,000 out-of-pocket annual limit, plan L has a $2,000 limit). Plans F and J have a high-deductible option. Only plans E and J cover additional preventive care and screening.

Each insurance company sets its own premiums (only the coverage is regulated). It is important to understand how your insurance company prices its Medigap policies, because how they set the price affects your current and your future premiums. Medigap policies can be priced in three ways: Community-rated (or no-age rated), Issue-age rated and Attained-age rated.

Community-rated premiums are the same for everyone regardless of age. **Issue-age** rated premiums are based on your age when you purchase your policy. Premiums are lower for younger buyers. **Attained-age** premiums are based on your current age (so your premium goes up each year). Premiums for these Medigap policies are low for younger buyers, but go up every year and can eventually become the most expensive. All three may increase for inflation.

Some insurance companies offer discounts to females, non-smokers and/or married couples. Some companies also use medical underwriting (you must answer medical questions on the application), and may refuse coverage or add conditions for pre-existing conditions. Insurance companies can't use medial underwriting if you are in your Medigap open enrollment period (the six months starting on the first day of the month of your 65th birthday).

The cost of Medigap coverage varies widely from around $400 per year to over $5,000 per year depending on your age and the plan you select. You should get at least three competitive quotes for the coverage level you choose.

Medicare Part D (Prescription Drug Coverage)

Medicare Part D went into effect on January 1, 2006 with the passage of the Medicare Prescription Drug, Improvement, and Modernization Act of 2003. Anyone with Part A or B is eligible for Part D. The coverage is being offered through private insurance plans that will be reimbursed by Medicare.

There are two types of plan D coverage: a stand-alone Prescription Drug Plan (PDP) for drug coverage only, and a Medicare Advantage plan (MA) that covers prescription drugs (MA-PD).

In 2006, the standard benefit requires the payment of a $250 deductible. You then pay 25% of the cost of a covered Part D prescription drug up to an initial coverage limit of $2,250. There is a gap in coverage between $2,250 and $5,100. You will have to pay all of the costs in that range. Once costs exceed $5,100, Medicare will cover 95 percent. There will be a $2 co-pay for generic drugs and $5 for brand names.

Part D plans vary widely, including what drugs are covered and how much you have to pay. They are complicated enough that there has been a lot of criticism of the plans because of the confusion surrounding them. Be careful. Spend the time to determine what plan is best for you.

Long Term Care Insurance

The average **annual** cost for nursing home care can range from $40,000 to over $100,000, depending on where you live and the quality of the nursing home. The average stay is from 18 to 20 months, and stays of 36 months, 48 months and even 96 months are not uncommon. A stay of these lengths can put quite a dent in most of our nesteggs. Long-term care insurance is expensive. If you have more than $2,000,000 you can probably self-insure. If you have less than $200,000 the insurance will probably be too expensive. In between, you have to look at it.

The cost and coverage limits of these policies can vary widely. They can be purchased at most any age (up to age 84). Coverage limits involve: the daily rate (maybe around $150 per day), the lifetime limit (maybe around 5 years, or $275,000), the "elimination period" (the days you pay for before the insurance takes over) can range from 30 to 365 days, an inflation adjustment (maybe 5%), and a waiver of premium (maybe after 90 days in the nursing home).

The cost of coverage like this varies widely with age. Premiums in the Midwest for $150/day, $275,000 lifetime limit, 90 day elimination period, with inflation protection might be on the order of: age 45 ($1,900), age 55 ($2,200), age 65 ($3,200), age 75 ($5,800), age 84 ($12,200). Most boomers have so far chosen to self insure against this peril – I have too.

Chapter 43
Retirement Lifestyles

Abstract - Retirement means freedom to pursue your personal goals, doing only what you want to do. No matter what your financial condition allows in terms of luxury, retirement can mean living life on your own terms and at your own pace. Freedom is its own reward.

Okay, so now you've got all your bases covered – **what are you going to with all your time!**

Retirement will not be the same for everyone. Some are hoping for a life of leisure, others intend to continue working in some way or other. Some are hoping for luxury, others only for comfort, still others are willing to live very simply just to have the freedom. Some have no intention of ever retiring at all (people who just plain love their work and entrepreneurs who have built businesses they love). Most people at least claim that they can't wait to retire.

Retirement means freedom to pursue your personal goals, and doing only what you want to do. No matter what your financial condition allows in terms of luxury, retirement can mean living life on your own terms and at your own pace.

In terms of work retirees fall into three main categories:

Not Really Retired – Nearly Full Time Work (with some additional travel and leisure)

My father never fully retired. He was the patriarch in a family-owned cabinet business in the Midwest. At age 83, when he passed away, he still spent at least a little time in the office most days. He quite simply loved his work and enjoyed spending time there. Many of you will take retirement as a chance to do some new work that is personally rewarding.

Semi-Retired – Part Time Work (with lots of additional travel and leisure)

The semi-retired baby boomers will have more options than those who have gone before. Retirement is being redefined by demographic necessity. In the next several years more and more boomers will chart a new course of semi-retirement by continuing in their executive positions on a part time (or consulting agreement) basis. Businesses of all sizes are losing their 'gray-haired' expertise, and are beginning to negotiate new ways of keeping them around at least part time rather than losing them altogether. This trend will be growing.

Retired – no longer working at all.

Some retire early, some retire late; but when they do retire, this group really stops working and shifts gears entirely into leisure. Once you retire completely (or nearly completely) you will be spending a lot more time at home, and you may discover that the division of labor around the house needs some rethinking. If you've never done anything around the house before, you may need to find a way to contribute.

I spent my first few retirement years in the middle group; choosing to continue working a little, while I got my bearings in the retirement lifestyle. I opted for the six day weekend, working only about three or four days a month as a consultant. Last year, I built our new beach house. This year I worked on this book and I'm playing a lot more golf. Next year, well . . . that's next year.

No one can be sure how their personality will respond to retirement. But the freedom to do only what you want to, at your own pace, and on your own terms is really quite liberating. Freedom is its own reward. Do as much or as little as you want. The choice is yours.

Appendices

Appendix A
Reading List and Web Sites

Investment Books:

Frank Armstrong, *Investment Strategies for the 21ˢᵗ Century*, (online www.investorsolutions.com) 1995-97; published as The Informed Investor, AMACOM, 2002

Peter L. Bernstein, *Capital Ideas, The Improbable Origins of Modern Wall Street*, Free Press, 1992

Peter L. Bernstein, *Against The Gods, The Remarkable Story of Risk*, Wiley, 1998

William J. Bernstein, *The Intelligent Asset Allocator, How to Build Your Portfolio to Maximize Returns and Minimize Risk*, McGraw Hill, 2000

Charles D. Ellis, *Winning the Loser's Game, Timeless Strategies for Successful Investing*, McGraw Hill, 1998 (revised edition of Investment Policy 1993)

Paul B. Farrell, *The lazy Person's Guide to Investing, A Book for Procrastinators, the Financially Challenged, and Everyone who Worries About their Money*, Warner Books, 2004

Benjamin Graham, *The Intelligent Investor*, Harper & Row, 1973

Robert A. Haugen, *The New Finance: The Case Against Efficient Markets*, Prentice Hall, 1995 (a great argument for value investing)

Burton G. Malkiel, *A Random Walk Down Wall Street*, Norton, 1996, 1973

John Merrill, *Beyond Stocks, A Guide to Better Performing Complete Portfolios*, Tanglewood Publishing, 1997

Jeremy Siegel, *Stocks for the Long Run*, McGraw Hill, 1998

Thomas J. Stanley and William D. Danko, *The Millionaire Next Door, The Surprising Secrets of America's Wealthy*, Longstreet Press, 1996

Ben Stein and Phil Demuth, *Yes, You Can Still Retire Comfortably*, New Beginnings Press, 2005

Larry E. Swedroe, *The Only Guide to a Winning Investment Strategy You'll Ever Need, Index Funds and Beyond – The Way Smart Money Invests Today*, TT Dutton, 1998

Larry E. Swedroe, *What Wall Street Doesn't Want You To Know, How You Can Build Real Wealth Investing in Index Funds*, TT Dutton, 2001

Larry E. Swedroe and Joseph Hempen, *The Only Guide to a Winning Bond Strategy You'll Ever Need, The Way Smart Money Preserves Wealth Today*, St. Martin's Press, 2006

David F. Swensen, *Pioneering Portfolio Management, An Unconventional Approach to Institutional Management*, Free Press, 2000

David F. Swensen, *Unconventional Success, a Fundamental Approach to Personal Investing*, Free Press, 2005

Retirement Books:

Mitch Anthony, *The New Retire-Mentality, Planning Your Life and Living Your Dreams at any Age You Want*, Dearborn Trade, 2001

Gillette Edmunds, *How to Retire Early and Live Well, with Less than a Million Dollars*, Adams Media, 2000

Lee Eisenberg, *The Number, A Completely New Way to Think About the Rest of your Life*, Free Press, 2006

Stan Hinden, *How to Retire Happy, Everything You Need to Know About the 12 Most Important Decisions You Must Make Before You Retire*, McGraw Hill, 2001

Marika and Howard Stone, *Too Young to Retire, 101 ways to Start the Rest of your Life*, Penguin Plume, 2004

Web Sites:

www.retireearlysleepwell.com
> The author's website for modern portfolio theory, asset allocation and retirement planning resources

www.dfafunds.com   Dimensional Funds Advisors (DFA)

www.vanguard.com   The Vanguard Group

https://bamweb.bamservices.com
> Buckingham Asset Management; Larry E. Swedroe; Fee-only-advisor (percentage based fees)

> Neuenschwander Asset Management, Roy Neuenschwander
> Fee-only-advisor (low percentage based fees)   608.838.8322

www.evansonasset.com
> Evanson Asset Management,   Steven Evanson, Fee-only-advisor (flat fees)
> Good overview of Modern Portfolio Theory

www.efficientfrontier.com
> Efficient Frontier Advisors, William J. Bernstein, Fee-only-advisor (percentage based fees)
> Good, very detail oriented newsletter (Efficient Frontier)

www.investorsolutions.com
> Investor Solutions Inc., Frank Armstrong, Fee-only-advisor (percentage based fees)
> Good newsletter; Great online book: (Investment Strategies for the 21st Century)

www.tamasset.com
> TAM Asset Management Inc., Jeffrey C. Troutner, Fee-only-advisor (percentage based fees)
> Great newsletter (Asset Class)

Appendix B
Glossary

Active Management: The strategies of stock picking, trading and market timing based on various kinds of research and information in an attempt to achieve higher returns than the market or market segment.

Alpha: A measurement of a manager's or fund's risk adjusted performance based on a benchmark reflecting the fund's exposure to the market or a particular market segment. The market or market segment has, by definition, an alpha of zero. *A negative alpha is underperformance. A positive alpha is good performance (better than the benchmark).*

AMEX: The American Stock Exchange

Annualized Return: The compound rate of return. See geometric mean below and Chapter 20. The actual average performance of the asset or portfolio over a given time period. Always less than the average (or arithmetic) return.

Arithmetic Mean Return: The simple average of a series of returns. The average of a group of *n* numbers, obtained by adding the numbers and dividing by *n*. The terms "average" or "mean average" are often used for the arithmetic mean.

Asset Allocation: The process of dividing one's portfolio up among various assets or asset classes. Fixed income assets and equities are generally considered the two broadest primary asset classes. Decisions regarding the amounts of value, small cap, international, emerging markets, etc. typically follow.

Asset Classes: Categories of stocks (equities), bonds and other financial assets.

Asset Class Index Funds: Index funds based on an asset class or group of asset classes.

Average: see arithmetic mean above and Chapter 20.

Baby Boomer: An American born between 1946 and 1964.

Bear Market: A period of time when the price of stocks drops persistently.

Bid-Ask Spread: The difference between the asking price (the price at which a stock is bought by a broker for an investor) and the bid price (at which it is sold by a broker to an investor).
This spread is the fee charged by the market makers – it is their overhead and profit; the cost of liquidity in our markets. The bid-ask-spread varies widely from large cap to small cap stocks and international or emerging markets. See Chapter 13.

Book Value: An accounting term equal to a company's total assets minus its liabilities.

Book-to-Market Value: The ratio of the book value per share to the market price per share, total book value divided by market capitalization. *Stocks with high book-to-market values are considered value stocks. Stocks with low low-to-market values are growth stocks. See Chapter 24.*

Bull Market: A period of time when the price of stocks rises persistently.

Buy-and-Hold: An investment strategy that involves buying assets and holding them over the long term and selling only for rebalancing or other long term strategic reasons.

Cap: See Market Capitalization.

Commission: A fee paid to a broker to execute a trade.

Compound Interest: Interest paid on both the original investment and accumulated interest.

Compound Rate of Return (or compound growth rate): The rate at which an investment would have grown (from compound interest) if the return each year was consistent rather than variable. *Return variability (volatility) reduces compound growth rate (the actual growth of each $1.00 invested).*

Correlation: The statistical measure of how strongly related two variables are. *If two assets move in exact tandem, they have a correlation of +. If they move in exactly opposite manner, their correlation is –1.*

CRSP: Center for Research in Security Pricing.

Decile: a sub-group including 10% of the whole group.

Diversification: Allocating assets among investments with different risks, returns, and correlations in order to manage risk and improve return.

Dividend: The distribution of earnings to company shareholders, usually four times a year.

Earnings: The net earnings (profits) of a company after all expenses.

Efficient Market: The concept that all available information is rapidly digested by the market and reflected in the market prices of securities. *Stocks with high expectations have high prices; those with low expectations have low prices. In order to make money on a stock, the company must do better than everyone else is expecting (not just do well). In an efficient market, research and analysis of publicly available information will not produce excess returns.*

Emerging Markets: The capital markets of less developed countries, such as Argentina, Brazil, Chile, Greece, Hungary, Indonesia, Israel, Malaysia, Mexico, Philippines, Poland, South Korea, Thailand, Turkey and others.

Equities: Stocks, real estate or other assets that an investor owns (as opposed to fixed income assets like bonds – where an investor, in effect, lends money).

Expense Ratio: The operating expenses of a mutual fund expressed as a percentage of total assets. *These expenses reflect the costs of management, research, overhead costs and certain fees. These operating expenses reduce net return. The expenses ratio does not include trading costs, which also reduce return.*

Fixed Income: Bonds, Treasury Bills, Money Market accounts etc. where an investor, in effect, lends money (as opposed to equities – where an investor owns assets).

Fundamental Analysis: The analysis of publicly available information, such as balance sheets, income statement and projections, and other indicators, in the attempt to discover "undervalued" securities.

Geometric Mean Return: The compound rate of return. The average return required each period for an investment to compound into a particular final amount. Sometimes called the annualized rate of return or compound growth rate.

Global Fund: A mutual fund that invests in both U.S. and international holdings. *An International Fund invests only in non-U.S. holdings.*

Growth Stock: A stock trading at a high price-to-earnings ratio (or low book-to-market value). *The market has high expectations for the growth of its earnings into the future.*

Impact Costs (or market impact costs): The increase in price caused by buying a large amount of a security or decrease in price caused by selling a large amount.

Index: A statistical model of an investment market (or market segment); often an imaginary portfolio of securities representing a particular market or a portion of it. *The most widely followed indexes include: The Dow Jones Industrials (the DOW), the Standard & Poor's 500 Index (the S&P 500), the NASDAQ Composite Index, the Russell 2000 (a small cap index), the Morgan Stanley EAFE Index (an international index) and the Lehman Bros Bond Index.*

Index Fund: A mutual fund that attempts to replicate the performance of a particular index, *such as the S&P 500 index, the Russell 2000 index or the EAFE index. Numerous other index funds track all manner of important market segments such as small cap, micro cap, value, international and emerging markets.*

Institutional Investors: Pension funds, banks, mutual funds, insurance companies or other large investment organizations. *Institutional investors are responsible for over 90% of trading activity in the market and therefore dominate the markets.*

International Fund: A mutual fund that invests only in non-U.S., international holdings. *A Global Fund invests in both U.S. and International holdings.*

Investment Policy: The stated (especially written) goals, objectives and strategies of an investor.

Large Cap: See Market Capitalization.

Lifestyle Overhead: The ongoing expense of the luxuries (in excess of basic necessities) we consume today at the cost of reduced savings.

Load: The commission charge that buyers of certain mutual funds must pay. The load is divided between the stockbroker, the distributor and the fund itself. Loads vary widely from around 1% to over 8%. No-load funds sell directly to investors without this commission. Loads may be front-end (paid upon purchase) or back-end, sometimes called deferred loads or fees (paid upon sale, or decreasing to zero over time).

Market Capitalization (or market cap): The market value of all of a company's stock. *Companies are frequently divided into large-cap, mid-cap, small-cap and micro-cap categories. CRSP divides market cap into deciles based on the NYSE market caps. Most stock indexes are cap-weighted, meaning that the stocks in that index are represented in proportion to their individual market capitalization. This means that such indexes are dominated by their largest growth companies.*

Market Impact Costs: Same as Impact Costs, see above.

Market Timing: Attempting to buy near the end of a bear market, or sell near the end of a bull market; or otherwise "time" trading to benefit from expected moves in the market.

Mean Average: see arithmetic mean and Chapter 20.

Mean Variance Optimization: The mathematical technique developed by Harry Markowitz for analyzing portfolios to maximize return and minimize risk.

Mean Average (also, Mean or Average): The average of a range of values *(not the median)*.

Median: The statistical center of a range of values that has the same number of values above and below it *(not the average)*.

Micro Cap: See Market Capitalization.

Modern Portfolio Theory: Risk management and asset allocation (diversification) based on the analysis of alternative portfolios composed of assets with superior interaction based on returns, risk and correlation.

Mutual Fund: An Investment Company that invests the pooled funds of individual investors in securities. Mutual funds may be either "load" funds or "no-load" funds.

NASDAQ: National Association of Securities Dealers Automated Quotations (the "over-the-counter market").

Nestegg (or personal retirement nestegg)**:** Your personal retirement savings – generally equal to your total net worth less housing, automobiles and other assets that will not be liquidated for retirement income.

Net Asset Value (NAV)**:** Price per share of a mutual fund (net assets divided by total shares outstanding).

Net Worth: Your total assets less all debt.

Nominal Return: Actual return, not adjusted for inflation.

Normal Distribution (bell curve): The familiar bell-shaped curve; *A graph of frequency distribution with an equal number of events above and below average, and symmetrically distributed.*

NYSE: The New York Stock Exchange.

Passive Management: A buy-and-hold strategy rejecting the active management strategies of stock picking, trading and market timing. Asset allocation to asset classes (as a whole) or asset class index funds.

Portfolio: The various securities or mutual funds held by an investor.

Price-earnings ratio: A company's market capitalization divided by its earnings. *The p/e ratio is an indication of expectations for future earnings. The higher the p/e, the more the market is willing to pay for a company's expected earning power. A lower p/e reflects low expectations for future earnings.*

Quintile: A subgroup including 20% (1/5) of the whole group.

Rebalancing: The process of maintaining proportional portfolio asset allocations over time.

Random Walk: The theory that future stock prices are unpredictable.

Real Return: The actual nominal return adjusted for inflation. Sometimes called inflation adjusted return. *The return of a security in excess of inflation.*

Regression to the mean: A technical term of probability and statistics. It means that, left to themselves, things tend to return to normal. *Returns, over time, tend to be subject to regression to the mean; that is, periods of over-performance tend to be followed by periods of under-performance, and vice-versa. Average returns for asset classes tend to remain stable over long periods of time.*

REIT: A Real Estate Investment Trust – an investment company that invests only in real estate.

Return: The profit from an investment.

Small Cap: See Market Capitalization.

Standard Deviation: A statistical measure of variation from average in a series of numbers, such as returns of investments). The standard deviation of returns for a security or a portfolio is usually a good estimate of its risk. Returns will be within one standard deviation of average about 68% of the time (7 out of 10 years); within two standard deviations of average about 95% of the time (19 out of 20 years); and within three standard deviations of average over 99% of the time (about 199 out of 200 years).

Total Return: Nominal return, not adjusted for inflation.

Tracking Error: The extent to which a portfolio does not directly track the market as a whole or a particular index.

Trading Costs: The total costs of commissions, bid-ask-spread, and impact costs from turnover in a mutual fund or any trading activity. *Trading costs are not included in a mutual funds expense ratio.*

Turnover: The trading activity of a mutual fund. The portion of a portfolio that is traded in a given period of time, usually expressed as a percentage per year.

Value Stock: A stock trading at a low price-to-earnings ratio (or high book-to-market value). *The market has low expectations for its earnings into the future.*

Wilshire 5000 Index: An index including all stocks traded on the NYSE, AMEX and NASDAQ. The Wilshire 5000 is a very broad index including over 6000 stocks.

Appendix C
Lifestyle Overhead & Compounding

From Chapter 2 The Power of Compounding

A Penny Doubled (every day for a month)		The $95,000 pizza		The $725,000 car	
		assuming 10% return on investment			
Day	Accrued Total				
1	0.01	20	120.00	twelve ($10) pizzas	
2	0.02	21	252.00	every year from age 20	
3	0.04	22	397.20		
4	0.08	23	556.92		
5	0.16	24	732.61		
6	0.32	25	925.87		
7	0.64	26	1,138.46		
8	1.28	27	1,372.31	a $10,000 more expensive car	
9	2.56	28	1,629.54	every 5 years from age 30	
10	5.12	29	1,912.49		
11	10.24	30	2,223.74	10,000	new car
12	20.48	31	2,566.11	11,000	
13	40.96	32	2,942.73	12,100	
14	81.92	33	3,357.00	13,310	
15	163.84	34	3,812.70	14,641	
16	327.68	35	4,313.97	26,105	new car
17	655.36	36	4,865.36	28,716	
18	1,310.72	37	5,471.90	31,587	
19	2,621.44	38	6,139.09	34,746	
20	5,242.88	39	6,873.00	38,220	
21	10,485.76	40	7,680.30	52,043	new car
22	20,971.52	41	8,568.33	57,247	
23	41,943.04	42	9,545.16	62,971	
24	83,886.08	43	10,619.68	69,269	
25	167,772.16	44	11,801.65	76,195	
26	335,544.32	45	13,101.81	93,815	new car
27	671,088.64	46	14,531.99	103,197	
28	1,342,177.28	47	16,105.19	113,516	
29	2,684,354.56	48	17,835.71	124,868	
30	**$5,368,709.12**	49	19,739.28	137,355	
		50	21,833.21	161,090	new car
		51	24,136.53	177,199	
		52	26,670.19	194,919	
		53	29,457.20	214,411	
		54	32,522.92	235,852	
		55	35,895.22	269,437	new car
		56	39,604.74	296,381	
		57	43,685.21	326,019	
		58	48,173.73	358,621	
		59	53,111.11	394,483	
		60	58,542.22	443,931	new car
		61	64,516.44	488,324	
		62	71,088.08	537,157	
		63	78,316.89	590,872	
		64	86,268.58	649,960	
		65	**$95,015.44**	**$724,955**	**new car**

Appendix D
Historical Data Series Composition

The following data sources were used to create the asset class and portfolio returns used in this book. All performance data are total returns including dividends.

DFA Portfolios

Fixed Income

DFIHX   DFA 1 year Fixed Income Portfolio: 1975-1983 DFA data; 1984-2006 DFIHX

DFFGX   DFA 5 year Gov't Portfolio: 1976-1987 DFA data; 1988-2006 DFFGX

DFGFX   DFA 2 year Global Fixed Income Portfolio: 1975-1991 Lehman Bros Intermediate Bond Index; 1992-1996 DFA data; 1997-2006 DFGBX

DFGBX   DFA 5 year Global Fixed Income Portfolio: 1975-1986 Lehman Bros Intermediate Bond Index; 1987-2006 DFGBX

US Equities

US Large Cap (S&P 500) 1926-2006

DFLVX   DFA US Large Value: 1975-1993 DFA data; 1994-2006 DFLVX

DFSTX   DFA US Small Cap (deciles 6-10): 1975-1992 DFA data; 1993-2006 DFSTX

DFSCX   DFA US Micro Cap (deciles 9-10): 1975-1981 DFA data; 1982-2006 DFSCX

DFSVX   DFA US Small Cap Value: 1975-1993 DFA data; 1994-2006 DFSVX

International Equities

DFALX   DFA International Large Cap: 1975-1991 DFA data; 1992-2006 DFALX

DFIVX   DFA International Large Value: 1975-1993 DFA data; 1994-2006 DFIVX

DFISX   DFA International Small Cap: 1975-1996 DFA data; 1997-2006 DFISX

DISVX   DFA International Small Value: 1975-1987 MSCI EAFE; 1988-1994 MSCI EAFE+ Emerging Markets; 1995-2006 DISVX

DFEMX   DFA Emerging Markets: 1975-1987 MSCI EAFE; 1988-1995 MSCI Emerging Markets; 1996-2006 DFEMX

Vanguard Portfolios

Fixed Income

VBISX   Vanguard Short-Term Bond Index: 1975-1993 Lehman Bros Intermediate Bond Index; 1994-2006 VBISX

US Equities

VFINX   Vanguard S&P 500 Index: 1975-1976 S&P 500; 1977-2006 VFINX

VIVAX   Vanguard Value Index (US Large Value): 1975-1992 Fama French US Large Value; 1993-2006 VIVAX

NAESX   Vanguard Small Cap Index (US Small): 1975-1990 Fama French US Small Cap; 1991-2006 NAESX

VISVX   Vanguard Small Cap Value Index (US Small Value): 1975-1998 Fama French US Small Cap Value; 1999-2006 VISVX

International Equities

VGTSX   Vanguard Total International Stock Index: 1975-1996 MSCI EAFE; 1997-2006 VGTSX

VTRIX   Vanguard International Value (International Large Value): 1975-1983 adjusted return from DFA DFIVX; 1984-2006 VTRIX

VEIEX   Vanguard Emerging Markets: 1975-1987 MSCI EAFE; 1988-1995 MSCI Emerging Markets Index; 1996-2006 VEIEX

Author Online!

Questions and comments for the author should be sent to:

info@retireearlysleepwell.com

Modern portfolio theory and retirement planning resources
including updates, articles, links etc. can be found at:

www.retireearlysleepwell.com

CPSIA information can be obtained
at www.ICGtesting.com
Printed in the USA
FFOW03n2054050716
25677FF